MAKING *Love* VISIBLE

In Celebration of Gay and Lesbian Families

Photos by **GEOFF MANASSE**

Interviews by **JEAN SWALLOW**

Design by **LEE SYLVESTER**

THE CROSSING PRESS INC. 1995

A trade paperback original from The Crossing Press Inc., Freedom, California 95019

First edition: June 1995

5 4 3 2 1

ISBN: 0-89594-778-1

Library of Congress Cataloging-in-Publication Data

Manasse, Geoff.
Making love visible: in celebration of gay and lesbian families
photos by Geoff Manasse; interviews by Jean Swallow.
p. cm.
ISBN 0-89594-778-1 (pbk.)
1. Gays—United States—Family relationships—Pictorial works.
2. Gays—United States—Interviews.
3. Gays—United States—Pictorial works.
I. Swallow, Jean II. Title.
HQ76.3.U5M34 1995
305.9'0664—dc20   95-6467
                    CIP

I. Manasse, Geoff, 1950- . II. Jean Swallow, 1953-1995.

THE CROSSING PRESS INC.

publishes many books of interest for a wide variety of readers.
To receive our current catalog, please call, toll-free, 1-800-777-1048

ACKNOWLEDGMENTS & DEDICATIONS

FROM BOTH OF US:

The making of any book requires a journey, some more literal than others. We spent much of 1994 traveling to meet gay and lesbian families all over America, and were fortunate to have been helped in that journey by a great many people. We would like to thank them.

Some people helped us find families, including Ellen Shapiro, Wilma Reichard, Veneita Porter, Betsy Walker, Scott Stalnaker, Craig Dean, Kit Qwan, Kenette Gfeller, Faygele Ben Miriam, Vera Martin, Jamie Lee Evans, Nancy Flaxman, Pam Slycord, George Rusen, Marcia Freedman, Carol Stephens, DeLayne Hudspeth, Earnestine Blue, Fai, Martha Reid and June Blue Spruce, Suzy Myers, Marge Mansfield, Len Hirsch, Fay Champoux, Stephanie Markos, and Debra Cannon.

Some people gave us a place to stay or fed us while we were on the road traveling, including Heather, Jim, David and Pam Martin, Chan and Edie Swallow, Sherry Emery, Susan Sanford, Chan and Tina Swallow, Herbert and Florence Manasse, Jurgen Muller, Sherry France and Naomi Almeleh.

And some folks found us families and took care of us as well, including Linda Bryant, Gordon Smyth, Wendy Williams, Austin and Cathe Swallow, and Jack Hafferkamp and Marianna Beck.

This book literally would not have happened without the support of these people. We appreciated receiving the name of every family we were sent, whether they are represented here or not, and every kindness extended to us as we worked to bring this book to print.

Several bookstores in the loose network of women's, gay and lesbian, and progressive bookstores across the country helped us too, especially the men and women at Red and Black in Seattle, Charis Books in Atlanta, Lambda Rising in Washington, D.C., and New Words in Boston. We value the good work of these folks, and all the others who work in that network, without whom books like this would not come to you. We especially appreciate the help given us in the making of this book.

We were fortunate to find publishers who believed in the importance and beauty of this book from the moment they saw the prototype: John and Elaine Gill of The Crossing Press have been willing to work with us as partners and we appreciate their support and expertise. Dena Taylor and Karen Narita at Crossing have been helpful to us as well, and we thank them too.

Lee Sylvester gave us a beautiful book design, which was important to us, but more than that, he brought our separate pieces together in such a way that they worked synergistically, the whole becoming more than the writing or the photos, could have been alone. For this, we are truly grateful.

FROM JEAN:

You will notice that many of the folks who helped us on this project are members of our blood families – they have been very supportive of this project. My mother-in-law, Mrs. Louise Walker has blessed me with her firm support, not only for this book, but also in my marriage to her daughter Betsy Walker. Her support, and that of my own parents, has meant a great deal to me. But without Betsy's constantly repeated belief in my work and this book, I could never have finished. It was too hard. I would have failed without her and I am pleased to acknowledge the importance of her support.

The chief text editor of this book was Beth Healy, who cheerfully worked overtime and without pay. In addition, the final text also benefited greatly from editorial reviews by Betsy Walker, Marian Michener, Cynthia Lindsay and many of the interview family members. I appreciated every comment. I was also supported at critical times by Tim Shafer who listened, believed and came up with some wonderful ideas when I was in despair.

On a project of this length, traveling so much for such a long time, working and living so closely together with another journalist required more patience than I knew I had. I thank my partner in this project, Geoff Manasse, for his willingness to struggle with me to the end. When we met at a party in 1993, Geoff was looking for a writer and I was looking for a photographer, and we both wanted to work on projects about families. The warm quality of Geoff's photographs convinced me to work with him, and I appreciated those photographs every step of this long way.

This was an extraordinary project for me. I have worked as a journalist for twenty-five years and I had never before had the kinds of experiences I had making this book. In almost every interview, someone cried, including sometimes me, and often people thanked me for their interviews, a confusing, transforming experience. Geoff and I were not able to include every family we worked with, but every family we visited helped shape this book, whether you see them here or not. I am thankful for each voice. The truth is, this book would not be what it is if the people in these families had not opened their homes and shared their love with us. For months, I tried to capture in a few sentences the essence of hours-long interviews, and I was often afraid I would not be able to do justice to their lives. If Geoff and I have succeeded in bringing these people to you, it is only because the families first gave us their hearts in trust. I recognize that as a gift beyond measure.

Without that gift, this book would simply be ink and paper. With it, and the help of the folks named here, and many not named, Geoff and I made something of value. I am gratefully in debt to all who helped us.

FROM GEOFF:

This project grew out of my desire for images which reinforced my joy about being a gay man. In April of 1991 when I was thinking about what was missing from my photography, my good friends Lyle Rudensey and Bob Allen told me how their infant son, Matiah, crawled into bed with them in the mornings to be read to. And I instantly wanted to be there to see it. They consented to leave their door open for my 6 a.m. entry, and from that first wonderful and simple act of generosity my life and work has been forever altered.

Upon the death of my coauthor, Jean Swallow, this book project would have been lost if it had not been for the pinch hitting of her life partner, Betsy Walker, and her dear friends, Marian Michener and Beth Healy. They did most of the editing. Laura Keisker and Kate Tossey helped by finishing some transcriptions, and Irena Klepfisz helped edit the chapter introductions. I have a great debt to them all.

DEDICATIONS

For my enduring family: Betsy Walker, Robin Walker, Kate Robertson, Gordon Smyth, Marian Michener, Wendy Williams, Susan Sanford, Diane Spaugh, Molly Spaugh, Cynthia Lindsay, Chan and Tina Swallow, Scott Stalnaker, Laurie Holmes, Annie Swallow-Gillis, Chris Gillis, Julie Holmes, the men I loved who had to catch the early train home: Nicholas Carter, John Sansoucy and Gregory Howe, and Catherine and Austin Swallow, my mother and father:

I love you all and each, now and always.
JES

For my Seattle family: my partner Dan Tuttle, our godsons, Kian Woo-Mintz and Benjamin Mintz-Woo, and their moms, Helen Mintz and Maylynn Woo.

For my sister, Robin Manasse and my parents, Herbert and Florence Manasse.

To the love and life we share.
Geoff Manasse

TABLE OF CONTENTS

TABLE OF CONTENTS

Continued

INTRODUCTION

Here's the story most of us have heard sometime in our lives, at least whispered, although recently the voices have been shouting, even down from the halls of Congress.

It's the story about lesbians and gay men. First of all, they can't have children. Obviously. Secondly, their own families kick them out because they are so disgusted by them. So either way, they don't have families. They live lonely, little lives singularly, with a stream of constantly changing lovers, in small, anonymous apartments in big cities. They don't have relationships that last, because their relationships are only sexual. They live alone and they die alone. They may have friends. But you know, friends aren't family. These people don't have families. They aren't like the rest of us.

Well. I'm an American, white, Anglo-Saxon, said Protestant prayers at night and at church on Sunday. And I'm a woman, middle-aged, raised middle-class.

I am also one of those women who, even as a little girl, was quite obviously going to be a lesbian when I grew up. On Kinsey's scale, I'm a seven, at the end of the range. And all my life, different kinds of people have loved me and made me part of their families. I have never been without people who loved me, even in the worst times: people from all kinds of places, some truly wonderful, some just plain decent.

So perhaps you can imagine how confusing this family business has been for me. I'm not supposed to have a family. But I do, and I have, and I expect I always will. And as I look around, I see this is also true for most of my gay and lesbian friends. And if I've been confused, if I've seen no words and no images of the reality of my life, I can only imagine how confused and how easily misled the rest of America must be about gay and lesbian families, how easily any of us can be made to believe that gay men and lesbians are, well, not like everybody else.

But are we? Are we so different? Aren't we driven by the same basic needs for shelter and belonging as all other humans, in all other cultures, and so make families wherever and however we can? The truth is shown in the pages of this book. Even though, as gay men and lesbians, we have been stripped by politicians, legislation, religious leaders and dogma, and rigid cultural expectations of the more conventional methods of creating families, we've done it anyway.

Here for anyone who cares to see the truth are some of the families we have made, armed with only our determination and our love. Making a family isn't easy under the best of circumstances, even with all the societal, religious, legal and cultural supports made available to heterosexual people. If it were, such supports would not still be so carefully tended, nor the image so selfishly guarded. The word "family" itself has come to be as closely guarded as anyone's home. But perhaps it does not mean only what it has come to repre-sent in this culture. Perhaps it is time to reclaim the word, and with it, a meaning that opens hearts instead of closing them.

In real life, people make families in every way they can, just as they always have. Married people. Unmarried people. Families with kids. Families without kids. Families with older folks in them. Families of a single generation. Blended families, step-families, my dad's other family, my kid's other house. Some of these families think of themselves as gay families, but all families have gay people in them, acknowledged or not.

So what makes a family? To begin with, love and the dream of love lasting. And then the second, crucial, ingredient: the acceptance of obligation. "Until death do us part." "For better or worse." We make these promises to each other, in a church, in a car in a quiet parking lot, or in the space between us as we hold each other in tears at a funeral. "I promise I will never leave you." "We will grow old together."

Love and commitment make a family. No more. And no less. No church ceremony or government document will ever stop love or its inevitable expression of honoring that love by our choice to shelter and claim one another as our own. And no one, no matter who they are in this life, no matter how much power they have accumulated or how loudly they shout will ever be able to take away the name of who we are together.

Certainly gay and lesbian people are not the first

folk to be denied the sanctity of marriage by both church and state. From the earliest reaches of Western civilization, we have records of those forbidden to marry: slaves in Greece and Rome, where the word "family" originates, meaning the household a patriarch owned, including women, children, slaves and chattel. More recently and closer to home is the example of the American South, where Negro slaves, forbidden marriage, participated in a ritual called "jumping-the-broom" to signify their intent to love, honor and cherish until death (or sale by their owners) did them part.

When we, as gays and lesbians, "come out" into our authentic lives as gay people, even when we are supported and loved by our biological families, we come to a new place, a place pushed so beyond the pale our very unions are denied the name family. But when we find love, when we make love, when we wish to build that love into a shelter out of which we can live the rest of our lives, that is, when we wish to make the commitment to marriage, the traditional name for the rite of passage marking entry from one family into the next, are we allowed that state of grace and economic privilege by church or state?

When we have children, are we allowed to keep them? If we wish to have children, if we wish to parent (that active verb), why do the church and state interfere in this effort to pass love, wisdom and care from one generation to the next?

And if we love someone to whom we are not married, someone with whom we don't live, how do we explain that person and why we might want to spend holidays with them, or care for them through sickness and in health, why they mean so much to us? If someone we love is dying or sick in the hospital, how do we explain who they are if we can't use the word "family?" Will we be allowed to honor our obligations or will we have to go to court to prove who we are, what we mean, what we have not been allowed to be, to say?

If you do not recognize my commitment, that does not mean I have not made one; it only means you cannot see it. And why would you be able to? Have you seen pictures of our families? Have you heard what our lives with our families are like? Would you know one if you saw one?

My family. The people on whom I can rely. This is the group I call to say Nick has finally died. I know they will understand that I can do nothing else, so numb, but whisper the news.

These are the men and women to whom I turn for nameless surcease, a hand held silently, a note in the mail, words of strength when I have none.

These are the ones I invited to my wedding, knowing they would come across country, across time, without needing more explanation than the simple act of my asking. And some came afraid, and some came in wonder, and some came in joy and some came in sadness for all they have lost. But those who came let me know by their coming who they were: my family. And when I walked down the aisle on the arm of the man who has loved me best in all the world, a gay man who is not my father, and I looked at all those people, I knew exactly where I was, and exactly who I was. I was a person who belonged to these people.

These are the men and women, straight and gay, related-by-blood and related-by-choice, who loved me back into life when my biological family left me. They are the men and women who stood

> *I'm not supposed to have a family. But I do, and I have, and I expect I always will.*

with me when my biological family tried to reach across their own pain and fear to build a bridge and when I was too stubborn to take an extended hand. They held out theirs until I could get mine out there.

These folks will argue with me. They will tell me when I'm making a fool of myself so I can stop. They will point out my weakness and protect me by helping me strengthen myself.

The men and women of my family. They have fed me when I couldn't eat, sheltered me when I had no home. They have laughed with me and danced with me and taught me everything I needed to know about being a decent human being, and they teach me to this day, every day, everything I will ever need to know about how to love.

They are gay, lesbian, and straight. They are old and young, black and white, men and women. They are all of these. They are not always there when I need them. But most of them are, most of the time, enough of the time, so that I know I can count on them, so that I know I have a home to come home to, so that I have someone to fall back on when everything falls apart, which it always does, eventually, doesn't it?

These are the people with whom I will rebuild my life, because that has always happened too. I have hope that comes to me when I believe there is none, hope brought to me in the tender hands of friends holding mine, in midnight phone calls from those who cradle my broken heart with their voices, and with this hope I can live, can do what is necessary to keep going. I have gathered these friends around me, across great distance and over time. I love them. They love me. We are a family.

These are the folks with whom I plant flowers and trees because I trust they will be there, somehow, next year and the next. They are the young ones to whom I pass my cooking skills, they are the old ones who teach me how to eat lettuce without getting salad dressing all over my face. They are screaming queens and military officers and the true sister of my heart; they are my step-son; the child I was not allowed to call my daugh-ter; the man with whom I wish to fox-trot for the rest of my life; and my partner, my spouse, the woman I married, Betsy.

This is my family. Is it so different from yours? Do they love you as much? How do you know?

I know because they have told me in a million ways. And perhaps those gay and lesbian folk you will find on the following pages will help you remember, or know, or bring together or celebrate the love that begins a family, and the commitment that makes it one.

—JES *January, 1995*

BEATING THE ODDS

KERRINGTON AND ALEXANDRE OSBORNE

San Francisco, California

Geoff and I were to meet Kerrington Osborne at his home in San Francisco's Western Addition, a neighborhood which has a long and rich history of a self-sufficient black middle-class, before the dream of urban renewal turned sour. Even today, one of the most beautiful parks in the City is in the Western Addition. Alamo Square affords sweeping vistas of downtown and a much-photographed row of Victorians. Less noticed by tourists, the park also has a set of very good swings, and a long slide – excellent for wild toddler energy.

As we arrived, the afternoon sun came full over the Alamo Square hill light and cool in the manner of winter in Northern California, soft but persistent, right into rounded bay windows of the bedroom of such a toddler, Kerrington Osborne's son, Alexandre. We waited there in the sun with him for Kerrington to get home from his work with the National Task Force on AIDS Prevention. Rosa, Alexandre's daytime caregiver, held him as the boy examined us through long lashes. He was not speaking sentences yet. He caught sight of us, buried his face in Rosa's neck and then looked back directly at us as she spoke to him in Spanish, and to me in English. He took my finger finally, wrapping his child hand around it, a gesture remnant from babyhood, but now quickly abandoned. He was shy, but not afraid.

His bedroom opened directly with double doors into the small living room, which was consumed by his playpen and his toys, pulled together for company, but clearly the focus of the family. Soon, he slipped out of Rosa's arms and showed me a favorite toy: a medical helicopter, bright red, lots of noises. Rosa stood near. Periodically he would run back to her and bury his face in her.

Suddenly we heard the downstairs gate swing shut, steps on the stairs, a key in the lock. "Daddy, Daddy!" he shouted as he flung himself into Kerrington's arms.

KERRINGTON OSBORNE

32, public policy analyst and attorney

"On October 24, 1994, I became Alexandre's father legally, as I was already in my heart. His mother is a distant relative who already had two children and was unable to keep a third. In 1991, I had decided I was going to explore single parent adoption. Ideally, I wanted to do it with a partner, but as 1991 came around, I was soon to be thirty and there was no partner on the horizon. Being a father was something I always wanted to do, and so I decided I was going to do it, with or without a partner.

"Wanting to be a father was actually something that delayed my coming out in a lot of ways, because one of the things I feared most, in my ignorance about lesbian and gay families, was my belief that as a gay man I would not be able to have children. The surrogate thing was happening, but I could see real problems with the contracts and it seemed the odds were stacked against me. I tried to find a wife for the sake of being a parent, but that didn't happen. By the time I decided being in the closet was not where I wanted to be, I had met more people in the gay and lesbian communities. I saw gay people who had children and my eyes were opened.

"Right about that time too, my two best friends from college got married and had a little girl, and I got involved in her life and later, her little brother's life. Just watching them grow touched that part of me that really, really wanted to be a parent. Even when I was a teenager, I enjoyed baby-sitting and playing with my younger cousins. It was fascinating to watch someone develop in front of you. They telegraph their thoughts and you can see their minds working. It's wonderful.

"When I was growing up, I thought everybody's family was like mine – parents were married for a long time; they both worked; they both were committed to their children and were involved in our school, our activities; and whenever we were

Kerrington chases Alexandre through Alamo Square Park.

having what my mother called 'family tensions,' we would sit down and discuss it. My father's an architect and my mother's an MFCC (licensed Marriage, Family and Child Counselor).

"I remember Mom would always ask about my love life. It's interesting how one is able to conceal one's sexuality by being too busy at work or at school for relationships. But as I began coming out, and started doing volunteer work for AIDS clients, moving from telling people I was bisexual to saying I was gay, I began dropping hints to them.

"I say now that my family's from Mars because when I came out to them on Easter Sunday in 1989, after a long conversation with my mom, her response was, 'Well, how does that feel? I felt like you've wanted to tell me that for a long while.' So then she told my dad. He called me later and said, 'Nothing's changed, we still love you.' My parents had always said they loved me unconditionally, and after I came out to them, my mother formed a PFLAG (Parents and Friends of Lesbians and Gays) chapter where she lived. Then she started a support group for lesbian and gay teens and she's been doing that now for a number of years.

"I asked her why she got so involved and she told me she had a lot of unanswered questions and she felt like she'd missed a significant portion of my life. My father has done some speaking on what he has called 'the hidden minority: gay and lesbian youth,' and when my mom told me that, she said, 'See, we're becoming advocates.' It was

great for me. It made me really value my family and it brought us closer. I've always been afraid I would disappoint them, and to hear them support me really renewed that faith I have in them, that some people do actually mean what they say.

"I think about my grandparents too – okay, different generation, small town Alabama, really active in the Baptist church – and my grandfather's response to finding out I was gay (he's like 81 or 82) was, 'What does that have to do with anything in terms of his ability to raise a child?'

"My mother called me in May of 1992, and asked if I was ready to start a family – she had found out there was a relative who was pregnant and wanted to place the baby in the family. When I asked my mother why she was calling me, she said she thought I'd make a great dad. Ideally, I wanted to have a partner – I'm used to having two parents and I think there were things I learned from each of them that were different. But he, as in Mr. Right, was not coming, and it was time. I was there in the delivery room when Alexandre was born.

"In African-American families, there is often a lot of informal adoption – we have lots of relatives we call cousins and uncles who were raised by folks other than their parents. Sometimes we were blood kin, and sometimes not, but for one reason or another, if there was a hard time in the family and the mother couldn't take care of the kids, somebody else stepped in. We've never had a concept of family where mom stays at home, dad works and

"Family is the folks who love you whatever. What makes somebody kin and not just a friend is about unconditional love. You intend for that person to be in your life for as long as you have. I've had to adjust that. I used to think forever. But when I lost one of my best friends, I realized I didn't just lose a best friend. I lost a member of my family, and my son lost a godfather.

"I want the world for my son. And I want him to have a sense of future. I would like him to grow up in a world where he's free to be a happy, healthy child, where his race, his father's sexual orientation, his own sexual orientation, will be factors of just who we are, rather than why we're bad, or why we're good, or why we're not as good. I would like for him to enjoy the innocence of childhood as long as possible.

"Raising Alexandre in this city, with all its diversity, and with the diversity of my friends, is giving him some of the diversity I got, although I had to go to Iran and Germany to get that full sense that cultures are not good or bad, they are just different.

"That's what they taught us. I've realized that the most important thing I can do in this lifetime is to raise a healthy child, both mentally and physically. People ask me if my life has drastically changed. Well, yes, it has. I'm home more. I cook more. But the main thing is that my focus in life has changed from myself to Alexandre. If I make a decision, be it around a career or if someone calls and says, 'Let's go out,' it's not just a matter of what I want to do. It's everything from 'Do I want to do this?' to 'Can I get a baby-sitter?' to 'Will this be a healthy environment for our family?'

"My extended support system here often makes me feel like I'm not a single parent. People tell me

there are two happy little children. I call that the myth of the American family. So for me, defining family differently was something that had already been done, especially for black people from the South. There is a notion that people take care of each other.

"Alexandre has in his family not only my immediate family – my mother and father and my brothers – but he also has a godmother here in San Francisco who is a straight single black woman. He had two godfathers, an interracial couple, one of whom just died, but he still has his other godfather.

it is so good to see a black man raising a male child in our society when everything says this doesn't happen. So it's interesting to find something that's natural for me is so remarked on. I think it's important for us as men to challenge ourselves around who is capable of nurturing, and what our possibilities are.

"Being involved in politics, and reading sociology and anthropology, I call it bucking the odds. I'm a black man who graduated from college, who's in his 30's and never been in jail, and I'm a black gay man who's still alive in my 30's. Some of that, of course, is economic, but I never bought those stereotypes of what black people were supposed to be like. It's not true in my family that men are not fathers. Even divorced or unmarried men, in my family and from my parents' hometown, were still fathers.

"I'm just doing what so many people do across this country. Single women, and married women who were really doing this by themselves, have been doing this forever. Men can be single parents. Black men can be involved in the lives of their children. And gay men can be tremendous parents. So much of it is really re-examining what the definition of family is."

COMING HOME

NATHAN LOVE'S FAMILY

San Diego, California

A family of seven, six adults and one child, live in the middle of suburban San Diego. They rent a four-bedroom house which is new and spacious. This wasn't exactly how they planned things, but the house is big enough for all of them. When we arrive, Nathan, two years old and just beginning to talk, is waiting for each parent to come home. First Sean, his daddy, arrives, then Kris, his mommy. While waiting for Lori, Nathan's birth mother, and Eddie, also his daddy, to come home, Sean plays with him, walking him wheelbarrow. Kris has gone into the den to see Scott Morton.

Scott Morton is very sick. The word "dying" is not used. His bed has been moved into the den so he can be with the family, but he no longer speaks. Scott Karatsanos had to stop working to take care of Scott Morton, his partner, and when they ran out of money, they came here, to the people who love them. Scott K. is one of Kris' best friends. Sean introduced the two Scotts. Together, Kris and Scott K. lift Scott Morton, help him cough, wipe him off. He's been coughing blood today, bleeding from everywhere. They lay him back down. Kris goes upstairs to change her shirt which now has blood all over it. Scott Morton will die four days after we leave. But no one is counting the days. Time is distorted when someone you love is dying: you think of what to do next and what will happen

when it's over, but it's too excruciating to contemplate the in between.

Meanwhile, Sean and Nathan play. Someone builds the fire up, although it is not cold this November night. Finally, Eddie and Lori come home from work, exhausted and drawn. Nathan is thrilled to see both of them. He goes up for his bath. Kris finally has some supper. Lori gets out of her work clothes. Eddie and Sean embrace. Scott Morton coughs and Scott K. talks to him.

Eventually, Nathan is tucked in, and the adults come back to the den, Lori now in her nightgown and slippers. It is past eleven. They joke, pass the time, until they go to bed and sink into sleep, the love of their family fierce enough to hold young life and death together in the same embrace.

SEAN MILLER

32, public relations

"I looked at the straight community and saw that people grow up and get married, and the husband and wife have a piece of paper that says they are family. As a young gay person, I felt very short-changed not to have that. I did the emotional exploration to find those elements in myself — commitment, love, trust, and patience — and I created my own family outside the legal bonds.

"My partner, Eddie, is my life. Lori introduced

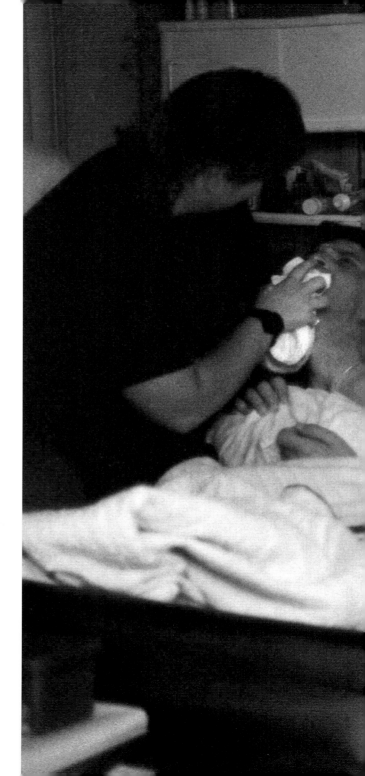

Left to right: Scott Karatsanos, Sean Miller, Lori Love, Eddie Blough, Nathan-Dane Melycher Love, Kris Melycher.

us. She and I met in 1983, when we were retail sluts. We were working in a department store and going nowhere, listening to the click-click-click of high heels down the walkway. We've been friends ever since. Our particular parenting family of Lori and Kris, myself and Eddie, came together in an interesting way. The night Eddie and I had our first date, which was June 18, 1992, was the night

Lori and Kris successfully inseminated. I was already committed to be the dad, and Eddie came into the role as we went along. Lori and Kris and I had discussed my becoming the biological father, but we decided as a group that a gay man who has been sexually active in the last five years shouldn't be a sperm donor, just to be careful. Nathan calls me 'Daddy,' and he calls Eddie 'Daddy.' He calls Lori 'Nonny,' and Kris 'Momma.'

"Also, right now in our family are Scott Karatsanos and Scott Morton. Two months ago, it became apparent to us that Scott Morton's worsening condition was becoming difficult to handle, with them living 45 miles to the east; a very rural state highway drive through sagebrush. If there was an emergency, there was no place to go. Scott K. needed to leave his work to take care of Scott Morton and that left them financially strapped.

"I've been friends with Scott K. for about eight

years, and I introduced them. They became partners and had some very good years together. We decided to take them in because we see them as brothers. We would have done the same thing for a sibling. These are two people who I love, about as much as you can love someone. I'm a few years older than Scott K. and I've always looked out for him, tried to help him.

"We had no questions, no need to talk about it — it was just a question of when we would take them in. This is not something I see straight people doing. It's not commonplace for straight people to have friends dying on them left and right. Straight siblings might help, but in this case, those blood siblings have not come to help. We are faced with our brothers dying, and so we respond.

"Family is who you would lay your life on the line for, those people who you would stop your existence to help. Our lives came to a screeching halt in September so we could help these people. They are my family."

LORI LOVE

31, medical administrative assistant

"I'm the oldest of three and I was raised in Dallas, Texas. My family is typically Southern. I always wanted to have children. I just love kids and family's the thing in the South. You've got to have kids! I was married to a man I met when I was in high school. But it didn't really work out. Sean and I came out together and we've been friends now for a long time. I always go to him for advice.

"I really like communal living situations. I like having people around and it's really nice to have so many resources; the more the merrier! Right now, with Scott and Scott, it's been very stressful. But I'm grateful that Scott has let us envelop them and be a part of his passing.

"Kris and I have been together for nine years now. She has this huge heart and just gives and gives and gives. I do think I'll be with her forever. She says she won't get married to me until it's legal. We were going to go to Sweden and get married on our tenth anniversary, but I'm not sure they'll do it for Americans. We've been keeping our eyes on which states are moving in that direction. I'm from the South and I think it's

important for parents to be married. It's kind of weird, but that's how I was raised.

"We (the five of us) went to my brother's wedding and my biological family were all very supportive. My mom calls and leaves messages for Nathan on the machine. And Nathan is such a good kid. He's so smart. Well, he's a genius, of course! I don't know how long we will all live

under the same roof, but I know we'll live close to each other so Nathan can go back and forth. I want Nathan to have a happy family."

KRIS MELYCHER

31, cook

"I never thought I'd have kids, but then my sister had a little boy and I just loved him to death.

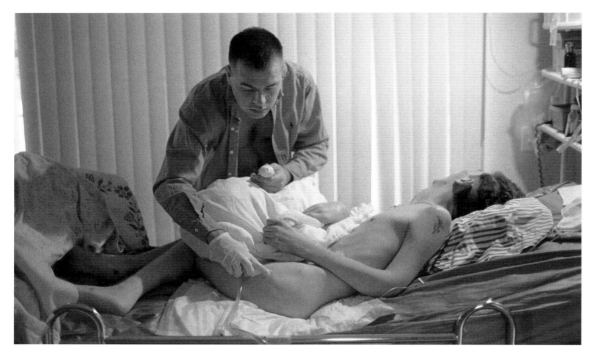

It was so fun being with him and we helped her raise him for a long time. Then it just seemed like the next step for Lori and me.

"Now, I wouldn't trade being a mom for anything. I like coming home and having him run up and say, 'Mommy!' And I like giving him a bath at night, and sneaking into his room when he's asleep and watching him. I just like everything about it.

"I would like Lori and I to be legally married. Maybe then my mom would get it. Maybe. She's a Jehovah's Witness. She thinks of Nathan as her grandson, but she doesn't see Lori as my partner.

"Scott Karatsanos is my best friend. Sean

brought him home one day and I just didn't let him go! Now, I'm really glad we can be there for him.

"Family is everything to me. I'd like to walk up to some of these people who say gay people don't have families, and show them a picture of mine, and make them understand they can't take my family away from me just by saying I don't have one.

"My father left us when I was about twelve. I guess he didn't really want to be a parent. But he missed out on a lot! I said to Lori the other day that I wished I could find him and let him see Nathan, so he could see what he was missing out on now. It's too bad for him. But I'm happy. I'm so happy."

EDDIE BLOUGH
28, medical billing specialist

"I come from a very average family. I've always known that I was different but didn't come out until I was twenty or so. Sexuality was never discussed. Neither of my parents is very affectionate. I came out at an interesting time, when the AIDS crisis was well underway, so there was a lot of awareness that came with that. And somehow that aided my integration.

"Lori and Sean had been friends for many years, and she helped push the romance along. In the beginning, they told me that Lori was going to have a baby, and that the key parents were going to be Kris and Lori and Sean. I offered my support to Sean and as time went on, I got more involved. It was interesting to be faced with some of these issues at the beginning of your first love. I always wanted a child and this was a golden opportunity for me. I didn't particularly want to procreate and put another child on the earth, but I did want to parent a child, to help him into being a better person. Now, I know that I'll always be one of

Nathan's fathers.

"At first, we were doing the commuting thing, but it wasn't convenient and it wasn't fair to

Nathan. So we decided to all live together. When Scott got sick, we just took them into our home. It's difficult. People are frustrated and tired and cranky, but we have a common cause and we do the best we can."

SCOTT KARATSANOS

27, computer hardware technician

"My former partner used to think that hanging out with family was boring and corny and stupid, but it's not. It's fun and entertaining. It's comfort. Family is about people whose shoulder you can cry on and they'll be there the next day when you need to cry again, not just for a short time. These people are more my family than my family is. I wasn't raised to be that close. I never knew how to share my emotions. Mostly Scott taught me. I had a lot of anger from growing up, and Scott showed me how to express it and give love and grow with it. Now he's leaving, but he's leaving something with me.

"Scott loves me no matter what. The biggest problem I have right now is what happens when he dies. I was never raised religious, so the theory of him going to heaven – I don't know. I don't know where he's going to go and it's hard for me to let go of him.

"I was really afraid I wasn't going to be able to take care of him, to clean up his vomit, his diarrhea. A couple times I couldn't, like when it first

started. The bed sores on his butt were so deep. Kris had to do it – she is so caring – but now I can do it. Sometimes if I spend too long taking care of him, I get too choked up. He still looks in my eyes and says, 'Help me.'

"These people have taken us in and charged us no rent. We have nothing. But I would have done the same for them."

MOMMY AND SWEETIE AND ME

TASHA BIRTHA'S FAMILY
Philadelphia, Pennsylvania

They live on a tree-lined street in a predominately African-American neighborhood, full of well-kept houses, all in a row. They are dignified old stone-foundation houses with waist-high fences around the small front yards, and the gates have no locks. Children come out to play with each other in a way I remember, but have not myself seen since childhood.

When we arrive, the children are not home from school, but later, when Geoff takes his pictures of the family on the front stoop, the children flock to him. "Show me, show me," they shout, and then surge forward into the frame until he has to ask them to wait outside the fence. Only Tasha, Becky Birtha's child, is allowed to go with him to the car and look at all the equipment in the trunk. Only she gets to touch and hold one of the cameras. The others look on in envy.

Tasha doesn't talk to them much. Perhaps it is the presence of strangers. She doesn't talk to us much either. She doesn't like to answer questions from anyone, Letha and her mom report, while we paint together at her little table in what was once the dining room. She doesn't much like to talk at school either, although she talks a blue streak to Sweetie, her cat. She escapes the painting table finally and runs off with Geoff.

Tasha has not had an easy life. She has been with Becky for four years and clearly the memory of the first year and a half of her life is with her. I watch her stop, review and consider those years before she says she doesn't remember much.

But without the questions, she is happy with Geoff and rambunctious with Letha and her mom. She is comfortable here.

BECKY BIRTHA
45, writer

"Tasha and I became a family through adoption. She was sixteen months old when she came home and now she's five and a half. I had always wanted to adopt a child, ever since I can remember. There have been times in my life when I wanted to have the birth experience, but adoption seemed like a much more meaningful thing to do. I'd always been aware that there were children who needed homes, and that a lot of them were African-American. I couldn't really justify bringing more children into a world where there are children who don't have families or homes.

"For many years I thought I'd adopt as a single parent. Coming out and living a lesbian lifestyle didn't seem to me to be a reason not to go ahead with that plan. I didn't decide to be a lesbian parent. I wanted to be a parent, and I was a lesbian by the time I managed to pull it off.

"It was pretty much a traditional adoption. I worked with the agency. A social worker visited my house. I did all the paperwork. They didn't have a problem with me being a lesbian. I had consulted with some other social workers and was directed to an agency where I was least likely to run into homophobia. I started the process in 1986, when I was in a major, long-term relationship. We were together for ten years, but she didn't want to have children. All the while I was with her, I put the idea of having children on hold, and thought I would do it later. But finally it was later. So I started the paperwork and then we broke up. I think it was one of the issues that broke us up.

"I did a lot of talking with Tasha about what a family was when she was younger. It's one of the things you talk with kids about because they're always talking about it in their daycare center and with their friends. It seemed important to get the idea across to her that the traditional heterosexual concept of family — a mom and a dad and kids who all live in the same house together — is not the only kind of family that there is. So, I defined it for her as three circles of family that we have. One of them is our household. Tasha would say there are three of us: me, her and the cat. To her, the cat is very important. Then there is the family of relatives: my parents and her Aunt Rachel and

Letha Bruce, Tasha Birtha, and Becky Birtha.

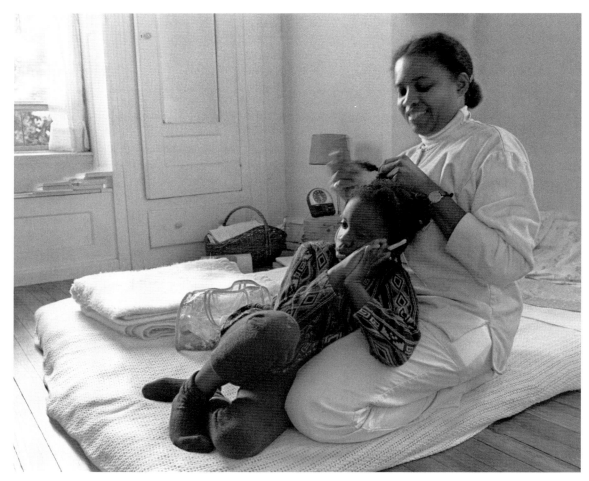

Uncle Eddie and the cousins. And there are a couple of other aunts – a great aunt and my mother's sister who is no longer living, who we talk about a lot – and some second cousins. And then, she has a family of friends. When she was little, she couldn't distinguish between who was in what circle, but now she can more often.

"Letha is a close ex-lover. Sometimes it feels like she has been part of our household family, even though she's never lived here. Other times, it feels like she's part of the family of friends, but she's the most important member of that family. She's never really become a part of the family of relatives, maybe because we didn't get married and live

together. We didn't have that kind of relationship.

"In a lot of ways, I learned something of what family consists of from my family of origin. My maternal grandmother came from a family of sisters – a lot of girls and one boy – and only two of them married. The others stayed single. Some were teachers, one became a professional classical singer and one stayed home. So there was a model of people not having to get married. With my mother, there were just the two sisters. My mother got married and her sister (Tasha Alfreida, for whom Tasha is named) never did.

"My sister and I are only a year apart and we were very close growing up. That's the ideal for the kind of relationship I'd like to have with a lover or a partner someday. No matter what happens, you know you're still going to be family. Since high school, my sister and I haven't lived in the same city, and that's sad, but we've always visited and we talk on the phone all the time. I really want our kids to grow up knowing each other.

"I've been out to my sister since the first relationship I had, in 1976. Her support was there from the beginning. When a family friend came out to his father, my father was very upset and said, 'I think it's a shame that this kid has never been with a woman and doesn't know what he's missing.' My sister and I jumped in at the same time. I said, 'Yeah, but you don't know what he's got,' and my sister said, 'Yeah, but you don't know what you're missing.' That was the first time I realized she was going to be an ally and it would be okay.

"The ironic part is, all the issues you need to believe in to agree with gay rights were taught to us by our parents. They taught us to think, to be open-minded people, and believe in equal rights.

"My parents like Tasha. Their relationship with her is different from their relationship with my niece and nephew, but I think that has to do with my relationship with my parents. I spent a lot of years of my life distancing myself from them, putting up barriers, and I think that made it harder for them to have a close relationship with Tasha. I don't think they have a problem with me being a lesbian mom, although I think they'd rather I didn't take her to the Gay Pride march, for example.

"For my father, it was a long time before he could separate gayness from sexuality. That made it hard, since gayness could be anything – it could be music or literature or potlucks at Quaker meeting. He just couldn't understand that when you talk about lesbian issues, you are not necessarily talking about lesbian sexuality. But over the years he's read some of my writing and met some of my friends and I think now he is more understanding. After we went on the March (April 25, 1993), my mother said she'd watched it on

television and it seemed like a really wonderful march. It was nice to have her call me and say so.

"Families don't just happen to gay and lesbian people. If gays or lesbians have kids, it's because of a lot of effort on their part, whether that's through insemination or adoption or through a custody battle to keep children from a previous heterosexual relationship. It doesn't just happen by accident the way it can for heterosexuals. These are people who value family and are really committed to making it work well."

TASHA BIRTHA
5, kindergartner

"My name is Tasha and I live in Philadelphia, right where we are now. Letha is my friend. She's a good painter. I'm in kindergarten. I forget the name of the people I lived with before my mom, but it was just for a little while anyway. I don't remember when I came here, and it's too hard to talk about.

"My mommy and my cat are in my family. Mommy and Sweetie. Just us. I like my family. There are lots of different kinds of families. Some are all brown and some are all white, and some are any color. I have a grandma and a grand daddy. They live in Philadelphia, too. I don't have a dad, and I don't care about that. I like living here and I like my mom, but sometimes I get mad at her. I can't remember why just now."

LETHA BRUCE
33, assistant editor

"One of the first things Becky told me, when we started getting serious, was that she was in the process of adopting and she was not changing for anyone. That was fine with me. I just wanted to be clear about what my relationship with the child was going to be. As a child, I had had relationships with adults who left and it was very emotionally detrimental to me. I had made up my mind I would never do that to a child. So I told Becky that I was either in Tasha's life or I wasn't, but we needed to make up our minds about our relationship, because I wasn't going to become familiar with Tasha and then leave.

"When Tasha first got here, Becky asked me to stay home for a couple of weeks so they could get

used to each other, and so I did. For a long time, whenever I would go to hug Becky, Tasha would put her hand out to stop me and I would stop. But I remember quite clearly one particular day, they had come to see me, and I had gone out to get donuts. When I came back, all of a sudden it was as though Tasha saw me for the first time and it dawned on her who I was. She ran to me and wrapped herself around me. She had never touched me or hugged me before. It took almost six months for that to happen, but the rest

Recipient of an artist's grant in 1994, Becky uses her time alone to write poetry.

is history.

"We don't have a name for me. I'm just Letha to her. I'm not really sure what my role is here. Sometimes I see myself as a co-parent because of decisions I help Becky make, like about Tasha's education. I haven't bought her a lot of things but I see myself as having a financial obligation and a lifelong commitment to her. In lots of ways, Becky's reactions are similar to those in my family, which is interesting, since she's black and I'm white and in some ways, our families are very different. Our ideas of raising children are very similar, so there isn't a lot of conflict about how to handle Tasha.

"I'm leaving to go to graduate school in the Midwest. Since I've known Tasha, I've told her that I'm going to leave for a while, but I'm going to come back. One night when we were doing the old bathtub routine, I talked about her and Becky flying out to see me and she said, 'And I will come get you and bring you back.' I almost burst into tears right there.

"Family has a lot to do with your commitment to the people you are involved with. It's a level of intimacy rather than the ability to buy things or maintain a household, which is obviously impor-tant, but not as important. To me, it's how in-volved you are in someone's life, in a positive way.

"There have always been gay families through-out the United States — women involved with other women who have children — it just wasn't called that. There's nothing to panic about. Most people have been living around us their whole lives — they just didn't know it. Now we're saying who we are."

Becky's sister, Rachel Birtha, with her husband Edward Eitches and their children Etan and Eliena.

RACHEL BIRTHA EITCHES

47, international broadcast journalist

"Becky is a year and a month younger than I am. We were always close, almost like twins in some ways. We often had matching clothes as children. My mother's sister was a seamstress and she made clothes for us.

"I remember being upset when I realized Becky was a lesbian. But I was also pleased she could talk to me about it. I think what most upset me was that I had always expected her to have a huge family and cook and sew and do all these child-oriented things she always liked to do. Here I was, not even married, and there were only two of us. I felt like she was throwing a fly in the ointment. I was mystified as to how this was all going to turn out.

"But then, she went out and adopted a baby girl. I wasn't surprised by that. She had always wanted

to adopt. She had studied early childhood education and I knew she'd be a good mother. So even if she had gotten married, she probably would have adopted kids anyway, because she thought it was a good thing to do.

"When Becky came out, I think it took my parents aback, and for some of the same reasons it took me aback. They tried to handle it with equanimity. I think my father felt that certain men had left her in the lurch at important times in her life, and as a man, that was distressing to him. He thinks that Becky is a really neat person, and he didn't want her feeling like a lesbian for those kinds of reasons. I think both parents now have more perspective.

"I read all the articles that say that lesbianism is biologically determined and that seems reasonable to me. It's not really something you turn on or off. I suspect there are lots of people who just never bother to deal with it, and go ahead and marry and have their families, but I think now people are exploring other possibilities. And that's what Becky did.

"To me, family is the essence of survival, whether adopted families or birth families or families by marriage or network families of association. There really isn't anyone you relate to quite like you relate to your family. So no matter what it is, I don't think people should allow things to come between them. You can get over almost anything, it seems to me."

A WELL-LOVED CHILD

MATIAH R. SHAMAN'S FAMILY
Seattle, Washington

We who live in Seattle in the winter need as many words for gray rain as the Eskimos have for snow. But come June, we are rewarded by an evening sun that stretches past nine at night, and temperatures hot enough to grow juicy red tomatoes and to cause grown men to splash happily with their children in the wading pool at Volunteer Park. On one such typically sunny summer evening, most of Matiah Rudy Shaman's family (his mother and father, his grandparents, his aunt and uncle, the two members of his family for which our culture does not have a title, along with his uncle's dog and several imaginary characters, among them Lion and Howard the Head) gathered together in a grassy meadow of the park to be part of the making of a picture of that family. There was the usual self-conscious awkwardness of picture-taking that showed up in bantering and shuffling, food-in-teeth jokes and position rearrangements by both family members and Geoff. But throughout, there was remarkable good will and patience, especially since it was the end of a long day, it was the second try at making pictures of the whole family, and no one had yet had a chance to go down to the wading pool. It may well be, as one family member said, that the comfortable familiarity of the group was the result of "incredible good luck." On the other hand, Matiah Shaman's parents have been very intentional about the creation of his family, giving the phrase "planned parenthood" a new meaning.

MATIAH SHAMAN
5, kindergartner

"I have lots of things and people in my family. I have two lizards, four tadpoles, and I also have some fish. And I have two finches who make lots of babies. (He softly sings this list, stops and giggles, then composes himself.) I have lots of people in my family, and they are: my mom and my dad, and Bob, and I have Lion (his mother roars softly and they both laugh), and an aunt, and I also have one grandpa and two grandmas. And Crispy is in my whole family, too. What makes family to me is, if I love them, and if they have been in my house a lot and I play with them a lot. Also anybody who loves or likes someone else in my family is in my family, too. Family is good for loving and care. I know that my mom and dad are gay and I don't care. Lots of kids' parents are not gay. I get to do more projects and get more good stuff than other kids. People at school don't know my family has gay people in it. Lots of people don't like gay people. I think that's wrong. Gay people are okay with me."

Left to right, back row: Willy (dog), Terry Rudensey, Ellen Shaman, Lillian Shaman, Barbara Shaman, Chris (Crispy) Beahler, Bob Allen, Lillian & Major Rudensey. Left to right, front row: Donna Shaman, Matiah Rudy Shaman, Lyle Rudensey.

Matiah lights the Hanukkah menorah.

DONNA SHAMAN

44, occupational therapist

"I was very determined about having Matiah. It's taken a great determination, and a lot of work, and a lot of faith. For lesbian women, you don't just get pregnant by mistake. Just finding a father who was a good person took a lot. My only surprises are the surprises of every mother: the aloneness, the intensity — so extraordinary, how the whole sense of yourself turns inside out. It's dreams and exhaustion and otherness in a way I've never experienced, an intimate otherness.

"I strongly wanted a man involved with my child, a lot because I loved my dad. According to my mother's reports, my father was very involved with us, for his generation. Mostly he was a gentle, kind spirit. I remember going to work with him on the subway, falling asleep leaning on him, feeling very safe and protected.

"It was a long process to find Lyle. I had already interviewed about seven or eight men, but from the moment I met Lyle, I liked him; I liked how he was with children. We got to know each other over long dates, but from the first he felt very familiar, and easy to me.

"Lyle and I have a legal contract where I have 75% of the responsibility and custody of Matiah, and Lyle has 25%, although last year he agreed to increase his financial contribution to 33%. Lyle didn't want full responsibility, and that was my first choice, too. When we disagree, we try to talk things out — I also try to choose my battles. But we are remarkably similar in our parenting.

"Lyle and I have become friends with each other. I love to watch him with Matiah; it's cozy and

loving and sweet. Matiah asked me once if I loved Lyle, and I thought about it, and I do. I was surprised at that.

"Matiah calls Bob, 'Baba,' and he calls Chris, 'Crispy.' He doesn't need a name for them; he's never asked who they are. He knows they are his, though.

"The non-nuclearness of our family is one of the strengths that we get from being a gay family. There is also an expansiveness, and a tremendous amount and breadth of love and attention by various people with their gifts and strengths. This is extraordinary and very stimulating for Matiah. With two homes and lots of people who inter-mingle but are also separate, Matiah gets lots of different experiences and an openness to the world. I think he sees a much bigger picture than most."

LYLE RUDENSEY
39, research scientist

"My ideas about being a father evolved from my job as a Montessori teacher. Every year there were one or two kids with whom I would fall in love and wished I could take home. My fantasy at that time was simple — that it would be neat to have a child in my life on a regular basis with whom I could do fun things. Then one day, a lesbian friend who had a child at my school called to ask whether I would be interested in meeting her friend Donna, a lesbian who wanted to have a child, preferably with a gay man who wanted to be an active father. I kind of gulped and then said, 'Sure.' The respon-sibility part was scary, especially because I was between jobs and not all that financially stable. But I guess psychically I was ready.

"A week before I got the call, I had heard this

wonderful report about gay and lesbian families on NPR [National Public Radio]. I remember I got so excited, I sent NPR money for a tape of the broadcast. Some of my excitement was just that it was possible, and some was the idea of being part of a gay family. I like gay people; I think being gay is fun, and it was exciting to think about doing family in a gay way.

"Family is a feeling of togetherness, a bonding with a group that is larger than just us, and lifelong-lasting. For me, family doesn't necessarily have to mean blood relation. I have a couple of friends I would consider family; it's just a feeling that the love between us is so deep I'm going to love them forever. You take on obligations with your family that you may or may not take on with your friends. I've come to feel Donna and Ellen and Chris are all part of my family.

"I would like to see Matiah become a loving man, whether he's gay or straight. I think that men in this culture really have trouble expressing love, and being loving. I would love to see him keep the affection that he has now for people and nature, and his ability to express that affection.

"A lot of gay people, because we had to work so hard to get to know ourselves, are more open and in touch with our feelings. That openness makes us great parents; we're already open to difference and have had to work hard on communication in our relationships. Children are a lot more sophisticated about feelings than we give them credit for. Also, a lot of gay people are in touch with their own kids inside, so we can relate to kids.

"I want people to appreciate us [gay people] for the special culture we are, and I want us to be appreciated for what we have to give children that is unique."

BOB ALLEN
50, draftsman

"I really like having a sense of family, a sense of there being something that connects Lyle and me together that is bigger than us, a physical embodiment of that. I feel I am sharing in something that is spiritually bigger than we are, than I am. I see myself as a sort of co-father. I don't want to step into the bond between Lyle and Matiah. I respect that. I oftentimes see myself as standing at the mouth of the cave, protecting what's going on inside. There is something about their relationship that is so incredible, I feel privileged just to be present. My involvement has come because both of them invited me in.

"It's an odd place. I'm not an uncle; but I'm not a father either. I serve some of that function when Lyle is not around – and Matiah responds to me that way. I'm his Baba. Now he realizes that every kid doesn't have a Baba, but when he was little, he just took me as part of the scenery. We were at the zoo once, and there was this gorilla group that Matiah pointed out to me. There was an obvious mother and child, and there was a big hunk of a gorilla he called the Dada, and then there was a fourth gorilla off to the side, and he called that gorilla the Baba. It's my name, but it's also an entity for lack of another word. We don't have a word for what I am.

"I would invite any person in this country to spend a day with us and Matiah and then turn around and say that gay people should not be parents. I think our family would stand up against any comparison of compassion, love, care, fun, whatever. And Matiah is a living example; he's just

a healthy, lovable kid. A lot of thought went into having Matiah, a lot more than ever went into having us. If God is love, then where love is, God is there. I can't look at my life and say God is absent."

CHRIS BEAHLER
47, librarian

"Donna was really committed to having a kid. I'd never considered it; I'd never wanted to be around kids much. But I got really involved, went through the whole process; I was the birth coach. We used to listen to him at night before he was born. It's an incredible experience; it was so real and so intense; all the externals were stripped away. It was this great adventure. I felt like we were a unit, we were so tuned into one another, so much further than you usually go in just normal conversation, welcoming this person into the world.

"When I got involved with the women's community back in the '70's, that was the first time I felt comfortable and able to relax in a group of people, feeling accepted for myself. There was a network of people around who would help you out when you needed, and you would help them.

When Matiah was born, there was something similar: real communication, where you are not your persona, you're yourself. Sometimes you don't know what your motivations are – you don't know if you are doing the right thing, you don't know if you are acting out of kindness or whatever – but in this situation, everything was crystal-clear. It was clearly our best; what we were doing was good, and basic.

"Matiah and I share humor and conversation about how the world works, and I love doing projects with him. I think of myself as his friend. He's the first kid I've had a relationship with, and he's opened my life up to other kids. Before he was born, I was delighted to find out he was a boy. I like boys. What I want for him is that he will be so sure of himself that he will not waver, and not be hurt because his family is different. I took a

children's literature class where we discussed that in the story of Little Red Riding-Hood, the wolf is not the only villain. The grandmother is a villain too, because no kid should ever be in the woods without knowing about wolves. If she had been taught how to deal with wolves, she wouldn't have been in trouble. So that's most important to me to impart to Matiah, that sense of who's a wolf and who's not.

"For adults, being around kids really softens us, and helps us to get in touch with the wonder of the world, and helps us live in the moment. A lot of kids aren't treated well in the world, and it's important that they know there are adults who might be outside the standard definition of family where they can get some kind of caring.

"Family is about the future, and about being open enough that people know your weaknesses and will not use them against you; you can be soft. Families are about where you get to be human."

ELLEN SHAMAN
44, curriculum development specialist

"I see myself as an aunt to Matiah, but also I am a support to Donna. I share some of the inconvenience and the worry of the child, and some of the financial burden. I was there at Matiah's birth, and I've been actively involved ever since. I see him a couple of times a

week, talk with him; I like to know how he's doing. He's a delight to talk with. The other day he told me that love is a feeling you still have when the other person goes away.

"These people are my family. It's not an intellectual idea. There are so many ways to love, and so many ways to make room at the table for everyone. I came from a very heterosexual world, although Donna and I are twins. I was the more conventional sister, always. I think it's important for someone like me, who not too long ago had her own homophobia, to say that she's changed and grown a lot, and to be included in a book like this. I think it's important to say that you can be clumsy, and change. I wasn't sure what kind of parent Donna would be, but she's turned out to be a really good parent. I'm proud to be part of

Donna's family. I love to be around that, share it with her and get old with her."

TERRY RUDENSEY
40, optometrist

"I'm the older brother. I must admit, I thought it was a crazy idea at first. Lyle can be really impulsive. I guess I didn't realize how serious he was. I was worried he hadn't really thought about what it was like to be a parent. But now, I'm impressed. I think he really did think it out. And I think Matiah has the best of all possible worlds right now. He has two households that care for him, and that's an advantage, because no one gets burnt out taking care of him. They get along a lot better than a lot of standard households."

LILLIAN SHAMAN
75, retired registered nurse

"Donna has a wonderful relationship with her son, and Lyle has been a wonderful father. Matiah is a loving child, spontaneous, friendly, bright and lovable. It's been fun. In all honesty, it would have been easier to have had establishment kids that went the same route. But now I almost immediately let people know, when we are talking about our children: 'Well, my daughter is an occupational therapist and a hard-working, single gay parent.' Years ago, I probably would not have said that. But it's a fact; same as if your kid got a part on Broadway, you would say that's what happened to that kid, and so I say what has happened to mine. Donna is a success as a single gay parent."

LILLIAN RUDENSEY
77, retired postal worker

"I didn't want Lyle to have a child. I was very upset. I worried who would be the mother. I didn't think he really knew Donna; all kinds of complications can happen, even in so-called normal households, and here was a more difficult situation. But now, I'm delighted. Matiah is just a marvelous child. Lyle's very happy and Matiah is the focus of his life, and Donna is a lovely person, and a wonderful mother. My advice to other parents who might be in the same situation I was in is to just trust your child."

MAJOR RUDENSEY
78, retired investment advisor

"When I found out Lyle wanted to have a child, I said, 'Well, this is a hell of a nice girl.' You couldn't want a better, warmer thing than they seem to have. Lillian, my wife, was worried, but Lyle was nearly 40 and settled, and I thought it was a great thing. Lillian swung over. In this kind of family, there are so many experiences that you never could get in a million years."

THE BEST MOM THERE IS

MARCELINO RAMOS, CAROLINA RAMOS, AND NANCY NOVAK
San Diego, California

Carolina Ramos invited us to join her family at home for dinner so Geoff has driven us down from Los Angeles and I have slept during the drive. I wake only when Geoff points out yellow highway caution signs posted on the shoulders showing a man, woman and child running, and later, white information signs warning of people illegally crossing the border. We are in San Diego, and I am disoriented by the heat and light and these signs on the highway.

By the time we come into Carolina's kitchen, Geoff, who was raised in Southern California, has on his shorts and looks happy. Carolina graciously offers us a drink; she and Geoff discuss product boycotts and I sit in the corner, trying to figure out where I am. The kitchen is only slightly smaller than mine at home, and when Nancy returns with the onions for the salsa fresca, I watch them bump into each other the same way Betsy and I do at home. Still, the light is so bright so late. Carolina is making us carne asada and the tortillas are warming. The refried beans are ready. I am touched she has gone so out of her way for us.

By the time I realize the next step is setting the table, Carolina is already calling for Marcelino. He is the same age as my stepson. He is on the phone. He has been on the phone since we arrived. She calls once, twice, finally tells him he must get off

the phone. I begin to smile; it is all so familiar. He arrives, a handsome boy, pouting like my handsome boy. I try to cover my smile with my hand and watch him. He begins to smile back. I ask him about homework. 'Don't have any,' he replies disingenuously, same as my boy. We laugh. Later, he tells me he wants to be an oceanographer. He shows us some breakdance steps, and we will visit his room where his mom has let him practice his art and use the whole wall as his canvas. He's a rascal, I realize as we leave, suddenly remembering my father's term of endearment. Filled with love for both my father and my stepson, I step out into the night, feeling right at home.

MARCELINO RAMOS, JR.

12, middle school student

"I live with my mom. I go see my uncles and my grandfather a lot because they are really cool. Sometimes I visit my dad, but I don't really like being with him.

"Me and my mom used to live in a trailer park in National City, but my mom wanted to get me out of there, because there are lots of gangs and stuff. I probably would have gotten involved with them. Anyway, she thought I would. So we moved here four years ago and I really like it here.

"Nancy's pretty cool; me and her relate a lot. We

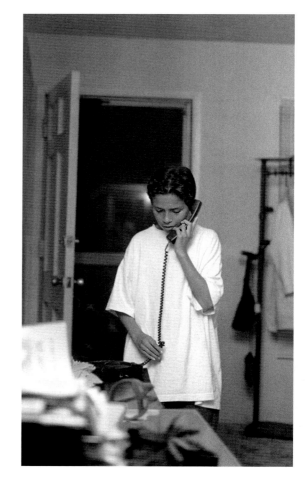

Nancy Novak, Carolina Ramos and Marcelino Ramos enjoy a family outing at an ice cream parlor in their neighborhood.

watch football and collect football cards, stuff like that. I tell kids she's my aunt. We have arguments, though, because she thinks I'm ashamed. But it's really because the kids at my school – they don't accept it. Nancy and Mom say, 'Oh, just ignore it,' but I can't ignore it; I won't have any friends.

"I'm not ashamed of it. At my other school, I used to tell everybody – everyone knew and they didn't care. But at this new school, they aren't like that. They aren't used to it yet.

"I can relate to kids having trouble with it, because a long time ago, when my mom first came out, I didn't really accept it either. It was new to me and I didn't know what to say. If I had to say something to kids about their parents being gay now, I'd say they've got to hang in there and give it time. Give it time so they can know how it really is instead of judging it really quick. Because for me, it worked out okay.

"Like when my mom and Nancy got married. I thought it was very weird, you know, two ladies getting married. I wasn't really fond of it. But then, I got used to it, and a lot of relatives came. It was on the beach and I gave her away, and it was cool,

but it was also really boring. But a lot of my friends came and we messed around in the water and the sand and stuff and it was fun.

"My mom has this group and you go and learn how to deal with your mom being gay. Like I play football, and I went to practice and Nancy and my mom dropped me off. The guys were all, like, 'Well, sorry, I didn't mean to insult you, Marce, but I thought that lady and your mom were going together or something.' I got real mad, and I just wanted to go home. I'm living a big lie with my friends right now. So I tell Nancy and Mom not to pick me up together.

"I don't know why people think that kids who have gay mothers are going to be gay, too. It's really stupid. I wish they'd just accept it like my other friends, and not even mention it. It's hard for me. One of these days I'm going to tell them if I get to know them good. And if they have a problem with it, then, oh well.

"Because my mom is the best. With a lot of stuff, she's real easy with me. She won't hit me or nothing – some kids, their parents hit them. My mom will just ground me and I like that better than being hit. And we talk about things. I like my mom being a lesbian better than I like her being married to a man. My dad drinks a lot and I don't like that. And I prefer to have women around. I grew up with it.

"She did get mad about my shoes, because they're Pumas. A lot of breakdancers wear Pumas, but she thought a lot of gang members do. That wasn't true. She works with kids and she asked them and found out it wasn't true, so she let me wear them. I'm not into gangs, anyway. I like active stuff, like breakdancing. And I like to draw and do art. There won't be gang pressure at the

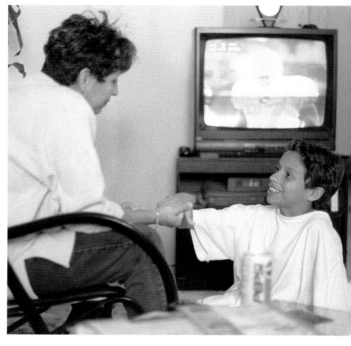

Marce offers to wrestle with his mother.

school I'm at now. Maybe at my high school, but I'm not going into it. It doesn't attract me – doing drugs, and killing people, and all that.

"I'd tell kids not to do drugs. Do art, not violence, that's what I'd say."

CAROLINA RAMOS, 31

childcare worker for abused children

"I knew I was gay since I was very small. I remember always having girlfriends and it was acceptable then; they all thought it was a friendship. I think I kissed my first girl when I was about 11 or 12. What we heard in our culture was that you

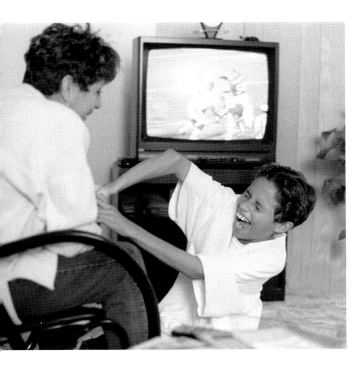

become a wife and mother and that was the thing to do. I just followed the program, so to speak. I did the boyfriend thing until I was 17 and I hated it.

"I was having a lot of problems at home with my mother and I ran away. I stayed at a house that was owned by the brother of my ex-boyfriend. It wasn't a sexual thing. When my mother found out I had stayed with this guy, she told me I couldn't come home until I married him. In our culture, once you have slept with a guy, you have to marry him, and I guess they thought we had slept together. So they took us to Vegas and got us married.

"This was Marcelino's father. I didn't love him but I was the submissive wife and did everything

I was supposed to do, and still it didn't work. I was very unhappy. When I left him, he got really abusive.

"What I heard when I was growing up was that the woman was supposed to take care of a man. My mother went so far as to tell me the first few years of marriage would be rough, that he would hit and beat on me, but it would stop. I said, 'Well, not me.'

"I finally got divorced and I started to slowly come out. My father, being from Texas, is a little more reasonable, but my mother, being from Mexico, has been the nightmare from hell. It took my mother a year to talk to me after I came out. There were a lot of threats to take my child. I was afraid of that, but I found out it wasn't possible, unless I had abused Marce. I knew I hadn't abused Marce. So finally, when my mother came over and asked me to choose between my life and my son, I told her I wasn't doing either. She was pissed when she found out I had investigated and that I had called her bluff.

"What helped me was that I separated myself from my family for a while. I said, 'You either: a) accept me, or b) I'm gone.' They contacted me after a year; they decided they needed me and wanted me back. Since I've been totally out, my father sees that I'm more happy and Marce has a more stable home life, and he told me that Marce seemed more adjusted.

"Nancy and I were really good friends before we fell in love. It was slow, but fun. The interracial part of our relationship has become a big issue, especially when it comes to co-parenting. Nancy's very strict. I'm finding that a lot of co-parents are

more strict than the biological parent. What it seems to be is the primary caregiver is not as strict. I believe in more talking communication. We've decided that I'll do all the discipline. Now, with puberty, it's been really tough, but I'm more tolerant of the stages of his growth.

"We've learned a lot from each other's culture. It's been hard, with a lot of changes, but we're getting used to each other. We really love each other but I always say love is never enough, you have to have more than that. So we have love, but we have other things too: being able to talk, and trust. When we have arguments, we follow each other around the house and we never sleep apart, no matter how angry we were in all these five years.

"There's never a dull moment around here. Marce is such a wonderful kid. We are so lucky to have a kid like him. One time, when I was doing a hate crime rally, he snatched the mike from me, because he wanted to say that he considered taking a child away from their mother to be a hate crime. He didn't want to be taken from his mom, and he thought it was hateful.

"It took San Diego a while to realize that lesbians and gay men do have families. I helped start a group for lesbians and gays called 'My Moms and Me 'N' Dads Too.' We now have over 60 families. When I came out, people told me I couldn't be a lesbian and have kids. And I was like, 'But I am a lesbian and I do have a kid.' Now I know lesbians and gays make the best parents. It's because we have to try harder to get our kids and to keep our kids, and also because we're in the spotlight so much. I think subconsciously we're very careful because we want to be the best parents we can be

to either: a) prove people wrong or b) because these babies are conceived out of love. Also, because we've been discriminated against as gay people, we teach these children to accept and love others, not to hate.

"A family is based on love, communications, fighting, making up, discussions, things like that. It's the love part, not the sex part, that makes a family. I'm lucky to have the partner and the child I have. Material things aren't really that important to me, but the little things, eating together and being together, even just agreeing on a movie, that's when I feel the family thing."

NANCY NOVAK

*32, Licensed Vocational Nurse,
studying to be Registered Nurse*

"It always amazes me when I hear about some people finding out that a date has kids and running for the door. Even with the problems we have had about stepparenting, I can't picture doing that. Anyway, I like Marce. He's very smart, and we're really proud of his grades. He could be anything he wants to be.

"Carolina and I are very different in our parenting styles but pretty much now I let Carolina talk with him. I understand where Marce is coming from, too, because I know what it's like being a stepkid. Sometimes I get upset because I can't speak Spanish as well as I'd like, but I'm learning more all the time.

"What I like best about Carolina is her stubbornness – no one can stop her. She knows what she wants and she goes after it. It's also the thing that drives me crazy about her. I think if we can make it through puberty, we'll last forever.

"I wish, when Marce went to school, he wouldn't be embarrassed by me. I wish he could say I was his stepmother. But I have to give him his space. I was going to volunteer to do sports medicine for his football team, but he almost got into a fight with some kids about us being lesbians, so I'm just going to lay low for a while. I just wish the mainstream wouldn't make such an issue of it, so our kids wouldn't have to suffer. At Gay Pride last year, some of the fundamentalists were coming out of the crowd and trying to grab the kids from the mothers. I wish they'd pick on someone their own size.

"Nowhere in the Bible does it say that God is hate. Jesus never hated anyone. Gay people don't go around trying to kill people or trying to steal their babies.

"One of my partners I worked with on an ambulance was a born-again Christian, and I was sweating bullets coming out to him. But when I told him, he was really good about it. One of his friends told him he couldn't hang around with me because I was a lesbian and so I was going to hell. But he told him I was more Christian than any of them, that I would give the shirt off my back to anyone. After that, I really respected him as a Christian, because I think he personified what Christ would have done."

When his mother is not around, Marce practices his break dancing in the living room.

EVERY CHILD A WANTED CHILD

THE GOLDSTEIN-PERDUE FAMILY
Worcester, Vermont

They live on a farm at the end of a dirt road in the region where Ethan Allen and his Green Mountain Boys fought the British so hard they created a legend of individually independent Vermonters. The Green Mountains are still as beautiful in the autumn as in Allen's days. There is high unemployment, but neighbor still helps neighbor. Every Wednesday, Cheri Goldstein and Holly Perdue's two older boys come into town to help make and serve lunches at the Worcester Community Center. The lunches are free to anyone, no questions asked. Kevin and Bobby are home schooled by Holly so it is with whoops and hollers that they leap into the van to come down to the center, free, if only for a while, of school tasks. They will sweep and clean and set the tables, chop and wash and do as they are asked, and in this way, participate in the life of the community around them.

At one o'clock, they will come home. By that time, Cheri will be home from her school, and will be studying. Bonnie and Karen will be arriving soon from their day program, and the two younger boys, who are still mainstreamed with one-on-one aides, will come home at three. They live on a farm, so there will be chores. They literally live in the barn—the hayloft has been converted to spacious living quarters with wonderful views.

Downstairs, the barn is still a barn, with chickens and sheep and dogs and cats and even a llama who spits if he is not let out each day to stretch his legs. So there are chores but also games. It is a farm, but there are children who live here, who play in the manner of all children, making drums out of whatever is at hand, playing hoops and soccer, and learning how to paddle a canoe. Learning, finally, that they are safe, and that here, every child is a wanted child. If they whoop and holler, isn't that okay, isn't that what Ethan and his boys did, not so far from here, not so very long ago? Cheri and Holly have fought hard for that normalcy.

HOLLY PERDUE
37, foster parent

"My childhood was very sheltered. I'm like that tee shirt with the person sitting alone in an auditorium and the words read: 'Convention for Adult Children of Normal Parents.' My father worked an extraordinary amount because he was self-employed, but I didn't grow up with any of the 'isms.'

"I've been interested in special needs kids since college. I did volunteer work at the local institution and I didn't think it was right that the kids there shouldn't have families, that you should house thirty or forty people to a building and have the staff change every eight hours and they didn't care whether you were clean or not, or whether you ate well, or whether it smelled nice or anything like that.

"I don't think there should be a child who isn't wanted, or a child without a home. I believed at that time it was just a matter of matching up people and kids. I mean, I wanted kids — why shouldn't everyone else?

"I was really angry with what I saw, and I was sad, but I didn't know how to make change. Now I can at least make life better for a few people. And by complaining and making changes within our local program, we can change the programs for the entire state. Instead of just thinking of these people as 'others,' people are starting to think of them as 'us,' and that's important. We could end up worse, with just a car accident or a stroke.

"Bonnie came to live with us eleven years ago. Her labels? We think she's alcohol syndrome, and severely retarded, but she's trainable. She's 25. And then there's Karen. She's labeled autistic and profoundly retarded. She only speaks in single words, sometimes in couplets. We think maybe it was birth trauma. She was given up for adoption 35 years ago and grew up in an institution. Bonnie lived in a foster home from around six or eight months old until she was five, when her foster mother died. Then she was put in a group home.

"I consider Bonnie and Karen to be our kids.

Left to right: Karen Henderson, Leo Perdue, Holly Perdue (in back), Kevin Perdue, Rici Perdue (in front), Robert Perdue, Cheri Goldstein, Bonnie Barrows, and their dog, Gisele.

'Kid' is not the appropriate word for them – Karen's only a few years younger than us – but there's no appropriate word for our relationship.

"Now, Kevin we've known since he was, like, 18 months old. When he was in second grade, his mother called me, frantic. Kevin was in trouble with the police for stealing checks. For years, he'd been wild, out on the streets of Montpelier. His mother has a heart of gold, but she doesn't know how to parent. She called on a Sunday and I told her that if she couldn't handle him, I would come and get him. On Monday, she called again, so I did. When he was in fifth grade, I petitioned the state to adopt him, since he'd been living here the whole time since, and his mom relinquished him.

"Bobby was twelve when he came. We were looking around for a tree-climbing buddy for Kevin; I didn't want to be the center of entertainment for a single child. There was a very large family out in Oregon that was breaking up. Bobby had been with them for eight years. He came from New York. Rici also came from that family but he had only been with them for a year and a half. He came from Mexico.

"Altogether, there were 93 children in this family, largely from foreign adoptions. They did it because they were saving the children of the world for God. They were Christians and did large amounts of fund raising, and they also got state money because most of the children were special needs children. Then one day, they decided they couldn't handle it, so they decided to get rid of all but twenty of them. So we got a call from an adoption agency that said they had a list of twelve little boys and which ones and how many did we want? The children had been physically, emotionally and sexually abused. Finally, the state of Oregon moved in and took all the children.

"The boys are getting better, because they know I won't let them get hurt. I told Bobby that if anybody hurts him, I'll hurt them worse and he knows I will. And if anybody tried to hurt Bobby, Kevin would either hurt them, or he would tell. Bobby told me that if they cried there, they got a cattle prod, the "hot shot," on your nuts. He's starting to cry now, which is good. I can be really angry at the people who have hurt Bobby and Rici, but that won't make them any better. We chop a lot of wood.

"So Bobby and Rici have been here three years. And then there's Leo, who's also been with us three years. What happened with Leo was, before Rici and Bobby came into the picture, we had sent our home study down to Virginia because we saw that they had a two-year-old girl there. We were one of the last people in consideration for this little girl, but they were really looking for a black family. I don't have a problem with that, because I think black kids should be with black families. So they asked us if we would consider a little boy, who was six and a half and had grown up in hospitals and infant care homes. We asked if he could climb trees. They said they thought he could learn.

"Leo was born at one pound, five ounces, to a seventeen-year-old woman who is now in prison for dealing coke. Having been born at 27 weeks' gestation, at one pound five, we can't imagine there weren't drugs involved. He was in the hospital for the first two or three years of his life with a trachea-stomach tube and 'failure to thrive.' And since he was disabled and retarded or whatever, the state wasn't so bent on finding him a black family, so he came to us.

"Leo's teacher says he walks into the room and it's like sunshine walked in. He's wonderful. He's not verbal, for the most part, but he understands. He's bright; he can follow directions and solve

problems. He can type on his keyboard and he knows feelings and emotions. And he knows what a family is.

"To me, a family is a group of people who take care of each other. It could be anybody. The thing about my boys is that they didn't come to us through a heterosexual partnership. That means that I had a choice and the state sanctioned me. Heterosexuals see that and they say, 'Oh! The state sanctioned that? It must be okay.' For some reason, heterosexuals believe that it's important to have the sanctioning of the state. I don't think that you need the sanction of the state – we sanctify ourselves. The fact that we make it through our lives every day and that we're successful, that our kids are happy, that we're happy, sanctifies us.

"There are lesbians who can parent and lesbians who don't have a clue how to parent, but who my primary relationship is with does not determine my value as a parent. Being a lesbian doesn't make it right or wrong, it only makes it harder. Other people expect you to be as good as they are, but in doing so, they expect you to be better than they are because they see themselves as being better than they are.

"There are people in town who don't like us because we're lesbian and some don't like us because we've brought in these children who cost the school district thousands of dollars to educate, and it doesn't help that the children are not all white. But Vermont people believe that you have the right to be an individual. So even though they don't like that we have all these kids that cost money, they still think, 'Isn't it nice that those girls take care of those poor children.'

"We're known as those nice girls on the hill with

those poor children. And it's true that we're nice girls, but our children aren't poor by any means. Our children offer more than regular people sometimes. Our kids, even Bobby, who's so quiet and withdrawn, offer kindness without judgment. They'll do their best to make you feel good. And they don't even try, it's just their personalities. For all they've been through, they are still alive and still willing to give and willing to try. They still have hope."

CHERI GOLDSTEIN

33, biomedical studies college student

"Holly and I have been partners for five years. Kevin and the girls were here when I moved in. It was a package deal: they came with Holly. Holly's the primary caregiver, but we are both parents.

"When we finalize adoptions on Bobby and Rici, they will be two-parent adoptions. When we adopted Leo, we had heard that there were problems with gay parent adoptions in Virginia, so we wanted to get him safe in this state before we went for two-parent adoption.

"From the time I was four years old, I said I never wanted to get pregnant. I never thought of adoption because Jews don't believe in it, at least not the Jews I was with. But I was really, truly and madly in love with Holly and so I decided I was going to deal with it.

"Now I like being a parent. I never thought I'd have a family to this extent. I'd always hoped for a partner that I could spend my life with, but it seemed like options were really limited, like having children. For me, family are the people who make my heart warm and are there when I'm empty. They can come and hold me, which limits out most of my birth family. I've been shoved out of my birth family completely, some because I'm queer, and some because the ones who can accept Holly and me as a couple, cannot accept our children. In my father's words, 'It's a nigger, a spic, a half-breed and somebody else's problem.'

"I expect to be with Holly for the rest of my life. I think of the boys as my sons. I don't think of the girls as my daughters – Karen's actually older than me. But I think of them as family. They take care of us and we take care of them.

"Rici was dropped on his head somewhere around 18 months old and had a bilateral skull fracture. We're working on getting his eyes un-crossed but being dropped also messed up his fine motor ability in his arms and his hands. He didn't seem to have the abuse at the old house that Bobby had to take. Rici is one of those marvelous kids that if something bad happens to him, he seems to be able to roll it off and look for something good. He wakes up happy and goes to bed happy.

"As for Bobby, he'll tell us that the old father would take a cattle prod to the other kids, but never to him, except we know that it happened. It's not all coming back for him, and we don't want it all to come back at once, but he remembers. He doesn't talk to us about it, but he talks to his therapist, we think. We had a sheep die here last week and when we were burying it, I asked him if he'd ever seen something dead before. He said, 'Yes,' and I said, 'Where?' And he said, 'At the old house. They were the babies.' So we know he's seen a lot, a lot more than kids his age should have.

"The older boys look at the girls as stepsisters. Leo plays with Karen; they have interest in the same toys. One day, someone was making fun of Bonnie, calling her retarded, and Kevin turned and said, 'Don't you call my sister retarded!' Leo, when he's typing out letters, calls us 'the mamas,' but we don't use that term with the other boys, because it was not an endearing term to them. We call ourselves Cheri and Holly, without a title. Leo doesn't have the bad mother figure–'nurse' is probably worse for him.

"For the first two years of Leo's life, he had a trach [trachea-stomach tube], and so never learned to suck and chew, things like that. My first task with Leo was to teach him to chew. I sat next to him for the first year he was here, like an hour and a half at dinner time, moving his chin around, forcing food in and not letting him swallow it right down. It was not easy, but he chews now.

"I cook for everyone, but we're trying to teach the older boys how to cook. I love to cook. It's my therapy. The older boys are supposed to each cook four meals a month, and it's been really hard for me, because I hate to give up control of the kitchen. When I lived alone, I had canned soup and tuna fish, but now that I have people to cook for, I cook!

"My family is eccentric, sort of a menagerie. Some people have called us the misfits, but I think we all fit quite well. I hope our boys grow up to be independent problem-solving adults. I hope to grow old with Holly and have a happy retirement."

KEVIN PERDUE

14, going on 15, student

"My family is Cheri, Holly, Bonnie, Karen, Leo, Rici, Bobby, me and let's see, that's all. Sometimes it's annoying to live here. We have to do these school exercises that are really annoying. They are supposed to make you smarter but they are very annoying.

"My biological mom is a lesbian too, so having Cheri and Holly as parents is no big deal to me. Sometimes it can be very fun and sometimes it's a bore. I like going to the [Gay Pride] marches, getting tee shirts, like that. I think they're good moms, okay so far.

"Holly teaches me at home now, but I miss some things at school, like driver's ed and chorus. I really like to sing musicals but a lot of people pick on me at school. They say, like, 'You faggot,' because they know I'll get mad. A lot of people here think that because the parents are gay, the kids are gay and are weird. It's stupid, but you can't tell some people that because they are bigger. I get into fights. And I get sick of fighting. What I want to say to those kids is, 'Get a life.'"

BOBBY PERDUE

15, student

"I live here with Holly and Cheri, they are my family. Rici and Leo and Kevin are my brothers. I had another family in Oregon. It was bad. It was bad for a long time. I'm glad to be here. It's better here.

"I go to home school and it's good. I'm learning here. I know that my moms are lesbians and I think it's nice. They take good care of me.

"What I like best with my family is when we go on field trips – Boston, New York. I like to travel and I like to go swimming. I get to cook and I like that.

"Kevin and I hang out. We play basketball. He's my friend. I had a lot of friends at my old house. I sort of miss them. They moved. I don't worry about Kevin not being good to me like at the other family. My other mom and dad are in jail because they abused me. I remember them. I'm glad I'm here now. But I wish we had a Super-Nintendo."

LEO PERDUE

10, student

"Hello, Leo" (spoken)

"Hello, Jean." (typed on keyboard that produces sticky labels that can be attached to paper)

"How are you today?"

"Fine today."

"Do you like living here?"

"I like living here and I love my mamas."

"What do you like best about living here?"

"I love living here just because real love is here. Love makes it. It is just important to me that people care here."

"Do you need to play with your brothers now?"

Nodded response, keyboard flung at Mama's lap, escape is made.

AN ALL-AMERICAN GIRL

ERIN FERGUSON'S FAMILY

St. Paul, Minnesota

It is a hot, sticky day in July when we come to St. Paul, the kind of day when you begin to think of air-conditioned places where you could spend long periods of time – the library, the movies, even a mall, if necessary. The largest mall in the U.S. is not far from the airport, we are assured, but we have not come all this way to see middle-class America in a Midwest mall.

We find the Ferguson's house in an older section of town. Built in the Prairie bungalow style, the house has been restored and, while not air-conditioned, is blissfully cool and dark when we arrive at mid-day. The three Ferguson women are home for lunch: Gloria, the mom; Erin, the graduating high school senior; and Anna, the younger sister. Buddy, the father, will be home later, after dinner.

We watch them make lunch—a salad, then cake for dessert. They each look so all-American I begin to think that perhaps we have come to the wrong house. Still, telling details convince me: Erin sports rainbow rings on a necklace, Annie has the graceful moves of the competitive fencer she has become. Gloria is so alert and so attuned to her children that I realize, regretfully, how rare this attention is.

Erin is unusual in that she has been able to acknowledge her lesbianism so young, but she is still a teenager, and she has teenage energy. Off in a rush to get her hair cut, she has to work at the bakery this afternoon, and then spend a little time with us — but not much, because she leaves the next day for her first-ever overnight outdoor folk music festival. After dinner and a walk in the park with her family and her girlfriend, she will gather up her other friends and go food shopping for the trip. It is eleven o'clock before they come home with food ranging from donuts to tofu. Her parents smile at me.

Maybe we have come to the right house. Maybe the truth about this young lesbian, who has won awards at her high school, is respected by her peers and her parents, and adored by her younger sister, is that she is part of Midwest, middle-class America too, all-American in every good way.

ERIN FERGUSON

18, College-bound Student and Bakery Worker

"As far back as I can remember, I felt really different, even as far back as preschool, but I didn't have any idea why. In second grade, I found out what gay meant from watching television and listening to my parents. Most of it was connected to AIDS, because that was the reason people were talking about gay people in the early 80's. I also got a big crush on my teacher at the same time. I thought I might be. But I convinced myself I couldn't possibly be gay because I wasn't male, I didn't live in New York, and I wasn't 25. It was the first of a series of convincing myself that I wasn't.

"I remember my friends getting crushes on boys and not getting it at all. They all told me I would some day. I thought, 'Well, one morning, I'll just wake up and will completely understand all of this.' But, of course, that never happened. I just went on making up excuses until I was twelve, when I sat myself down and said, 'Well, this has been going on for a long time and maybe I am gay.' That was a tremendous relief. But then it occurred to me that I had to tell other people, and that sense of relief just fled.

"The first people I thought to tell were my parents, since that's who I was mainly talking to because I was twelve, but over the years I had picked up that a lot of parents aren't too keen on the idea of having a gay kid. So I decided to wait a year, and if I was still gay in a year, I would tell my family, because everything you do when you are twelve is a phase. I didn't want to come back three weeks later and say, 'Just kidding.'

"So I waited the year, and tried to suck in every piece of information I could get about gay people. That year came and went and I was still gay, and I kept meaning to tell them and meaning to tell them,

Buddy, Gloria, Erin, and Anna Ferguson relax after an evening walk around the lake.

Preparing a lunch time salad, Erin jokes with her mother.

wasn't. I was just mostly going to eighth grade. Since the support group got started, the climate at my high school has completely turned around. Because I had the support group, I felt more comfortable being out and being a role model. By the time I finished my freshman year, everybody knew I was gay and everybody was fine with it. I mean, there have been little incidents, but they've been so minor compared to the support that it hasn't been an issue. I've been out for five years, and an activist for four years, and I've only gotten four pieces of hate mail.

"Like last year, we decided to have a gay booth at the multi-cultural festival we have at school. So we approached the organizers and they said they didn't think it would be such a good idea because it might upset the parents. But there was a school policy that said they couldn't discriminate on the basis of sexual orientation, so we went back and said, 'No, you don't understand. You have to let us have this booth.' The decision got delegated to the principal who said, 'No.' So we got together with a lawyer who wrote a bunch of scary letters to everybody. It became really clear that who wasn't on our side were a few people in the administration. Even the people who weren't originally on our side got behind us. Kids were coming in and saying if we weren't allowed in, they would pull their booths out. Lots of teachers came forward and said they thought it was wrong. Finally, the principal got ordered to let us in. And it was a big success. We served quiche and played tapes by the Village People.

"I met Rose in English class. I spotted her right away and moved near where she was sitting. But she was really shy and I had to talk to about 30 of her friends before I actually got to talk to her. I started to go to a women's issues group because she was in it, and she finally came down to a place where I was volunteering. We started going out after we tried to sue our principal together. I asked her out – I can't imagine Rose asking me out; she's rather reserved, but in a very cute way. We've been going out for more than a year, and I guess we're going steady.

"Unlike a lot of gay and lesbian people, I've never

but I kept having this huge anxiety attack. I knew them well enough to know they would probably be fine with it, but I also knew what the opposite extreme was, and I was not ready to be kicked out of my house.

"When I finally told my mom, she freaked out for about five minutes, but that was all. My dad had already figured it out long before I had, and Anna didn't have any concept of how weird anything was, so she's always been fine with it. One of the nice things my mom did was that she understood that having adult gay friends was not the same as having gay friends my own age, and so she started looking around for a support group for me. She ended up getting everything set up for me.

"When I tell my story this way, and condense it like this, it all sounds so dramatic, but it really

Erin and Anna find Anna's name in a fencing magazine.

Erin on the bed in her room in the summer between high school and college.

sort of grow up and become my parents, get married in the Unitarian church, and so I guess I will. But you know, I'm only 18 and it's special if I know what I'm doing for the weekend. I can't plan that far ahead."

GLORIA FERGUSON

44, Health Educator

"When Erin was in seventh grade, I noticed that all of her friends were putting on make-up and jacking up their bangs, and obviously interested in boys. And Erin was not. I remember saying to a friend of mine at work, 'Gee, Erin's not interested in boys. I wonder whether she's going to be interested in boys, or maybe she's lesbian.' My friend asked, 'Well, how would it be for you if she were?' I said, 'I have no problem with that, but it seems like a harder life than being a straight kid, and I don't want a harder life for my child.' The next year, Erin came out.

"The way that happened was Erin and Annie and I were sitting at the dinner table. My husband tends to work late; he's usually not home until after eight. We were having Chinese food take-out, which is something we do often. Erin was eating lemon chicken and Annie said, 'Gee, Erin is really hungry tonight.' Erin looked at me and said, 'And I'm also gay.'

"I said, 'What?' and she said, 'I'm also gay.' I said, 'Well, are you sure? Because lots of people your age feel closer to girls than to boys.' And she just said, 'Yes, I'm sure.' That's one thing I regret saying now, because when I told my mother I was going to go out on a date with a boy, she never said, 'Well, are you sure you're straight, honey?'

"But that evening, that was about all Erin could stand, and she said, 'Well, I'm going to go do my

really had to look for much outside my family. When I came out there were all these wonderful gay and lesbian adults who came forward and said, 'Good, you're finally here. Welcome home.' That's my community and my culture, and where I feel I belong, but I don't feel my family is separate from that. As much as any straight people can, my parents have completely immersed themselves in my culture. They go to the movies, they read the books,

they get the jokes. They went to the March on Washington with me. Being a lesbian is the best thing that ever happened to me; it's a wonderful culture to be a part of.

"My parents are really mature and they've thought about things in a really healthy way, and I'm proud of them. Sometimes, they embarrass me, but I feel like it's worth it, to have parents as together as they are. I always pictured that I would

Stephen and I was shaking. Finally, Stephen said the most wonderful thing: 'You know Gloria, I have two straight sisters and a straight brother and my life is as good or better than any of theirs. And Erin has a nice family and good friends, and she's going to be fine.' I sat and cried for a while, and I thought, 'Well, Erin is a really strong person, and an intelligent person, and she is going to be fine. I think.'

homework now.' I said, 'Well, I love you.' She went to her room, and I went upstairs and called my gay friend who lives next door, Stephen. I said, 'Stephen, Erin just came out.' He asked me how I felt, and I said I was really scared, because I was; that was my first reaction. It reminded me of a time when Erin was really little and I was home doing daycare. One day she and her friend Sam were walking home from school and Sam came running in the kitchen and said, 'Some girls are beating up on Erin.' It was like mother bear came out. I just dropped everything and ran to the corner. I took this girl by the lapels and said, 'Don't you ever bother my child again!'

"I wanted to do that to the world when Erin came out. It wasn't that I wanted to change her; I wanted to change the world and say, 'Leave my kid alone!' I just sat there on the phone with

"I wasn't sure at that point what people's reaction would be, and how safe it would be to tell people. I was scared about not telling people, about making her hide or encouraging her to hide, so she'd stay safe. But it isn't safe to hide either, and it felt like we had to choose between living her life and physical safety. But that turned out to be not the choice at all.

"Later on Buddy came home and I told him. He just smiled and said it had occurred to him before. Gradually, we told friends, and they were wonderful and welcoming. The next summer, some friends of ours invited Erin to come with them and a lesbian couple who were friends of theirs on a canoe trip, because they wanted her to see a nice lesbian couple who had been together for a long time. So Erin went and had a good time.

"I also looked for a support group for my 13-year-old daughter. Mostly there were groups for guys who were 18 or 19 years old. There wasn't a group for Erin, so I went to a school nurse I knew who was supportive and I asked her if she would support a group at her school. She worked with the high school clinic staff. Erin requested it in September, and by October, it was started.

"I think my having gay friends made it somewhat easier for Erin; she knew I was comfortable talking about sexuality, but it still took her a year between the time she came out to herself and the time she came out to us, which really says a lot to me about how frightening a process coming out is. Every once in a while now, a parent will call me and say, 'I think my child is gay – what should I do? I want to let her know that it's okay. Should I just tell her?' And I say, 'No. Tell her in other ways. Pick up the paper and say, "Look at the good news about Margarethe Cammermeyer," or, "Look at this terrible thing in the military," but don't confront them'. People just have to go through that internal process in their own time.

"People identify me as the parent of a gay child, and it feels good to me. I think one of the biggest things that maintains ignorance and insensitivity is invisibility. So if people see me as Erin's mom, and see her as a good person who is also lesbian, then it makes me happy. I like to be visible to kids in my high school, so they can come talk, if they want. And they do.

"It's total bullshit to think something parents did made their child gay. With Erin, from the day she was born, she was a unique individual. She was my first, so I didn't know how unique she was, but she was a kid who was always much more comfortable

in her overalls. I think homosexuality must be genetic; the only choice is whether you live true to your being or you don't.

"It always surprises me when I hear about gay people being disowned by their families. It is absolutely beyond my understanding. If you loved each other before, why would you stop? Is it fear that gets magnified so much people can't deal with it? What a sad thing to lose a child, and by your own will – unimaginable. It's also sad when people just see it as, 'Well, here's my kid, and yeah, she's lesbian, but that doesn't really matter.' It does matter.

"It's so sad when these things happen, because you miss out on all the good stuff – not just the good stuff of being somebody's mom, which is the best part of my life, but you also miss out on the good stuff of being part of the gay and lesbian community, which is fun. A big part of life is being connected to other people in some meaningful way, and I think if it hadn't been for Erin being who she is, we would have passed by this whole part of humanity, without taking much of a second look.

"I've done a lot of thinking about where that fear comes from because when I was growing up, people didn't talk about this. You didn't even hear the words. I think the fear is fed to us in our mashed potatoes. It's a kind of discrimination that we don't even know we have. So I guess in that way, people's reactions are not so surprising, but once you get through it, the support and love that can come from friends and family and even strangers can be such a blessing and overwhelmingly lovely.

"It hasn't all been positive for Erin. The things that have been difficult are other people's anger, or when Clinton went back on his promise about gays in the military, or when I tried to put up posters about support groups and was told by people that it would create danger for the students, or when Erin gets hate mail. The anger has, at times, been so overwhelming I wonder how people live with it day to day, but I've come to a better understanding of what discrimination and prejudice mean. I think if people have personal experience with that level of bigotry, they are less likely to dish it out to other people.

"I have come to see myself as different, but only because people tell me so. I come from an ordinary family and I certainly don't see myself as a remarkable parent. I think there are probably lots of parents who feel the way I do about their gay children, but haven't had the forum I have had to say so.

"Once I heard a father say, after his son came out to him, that he wanted his 'other' son back. There is a sense of loss when your child comes out, but what you are losing is the illusion of safety, the idea that we can protect our children. To have all the ugliness about gay and lesbian people that is always out there, and that we have taken in, come in our faces when our children come out, takes a while to recover from.

"We get our children back when they get to be who they are. When Erin wasn't able to come out yet, I remember one day walking down the sidewalk with her and wanting to put my arm around her shoulder and she wouldn't let me. But now I can. We don't get to make our kids be who we want them to be and it's a darn good thing. I couldn't have imagined anything as beautiful as my children."

Rose Stenglein, Elizabeth Shreve, Erin Ferguson, and Marta Murray-Close buy groceries for a weekend outing to a music festival.

BUDDY FERGUSON

47, public information officer,
Minnesota Health Department

"Before Erin came out, I was worried about her because she seemed to be going through that awkward stage of early high school and adolescence with unusual awkwardness. This was in a kid who had an uncanny poise about herself when she was a child, very self-assured and self-contained. She seemed to be hiding something, and wore dark, baggy clothes. She seemed to be hanging on to childhood in some way I couldn't define. But when she came out, all that fell away and her poise came back and she developed a sense of style about herself.

"I don't think it's true that girls become lesbians because they don't have a good relationship with their fathers. I've always felt quite close to Erin. There was a period after Erin was born when I was staying home with her and I wouldn't have traded that time for anything. Erin and I share a certain sense of humor and an interest in politics and social awareness.

"Erin has always been a very resilient kid in many ways, and it's one of the reasons I was able to sweep aside some of the fears I had about what

Erin at her part time job in a bakery wraps bread.

might happen to her because she's lesbian. I had faith in her ability to cope with things and land with her feet on the ground.

"It was a great experience to go to the National March on Washington last year. Erin wanted to go, and we all decided it would be fun, if that's not too frivolous a word. It had sort of a '60s feel about it, a sense of idealism and purpose, and commitment to something so straightforward. That is hard to come by in our culture at this point in time; there seems to be a kind of compulsive cynicism that wasn't true that weekend. I felt buoyed by the whole thing. It was joyful and exuberant and very positive.

"I'm accommodating myself to the fact Erin is essentially an adult now. I'm looking forward to the future and who she will become. I'd like her to have happiness above all. She's a really great kid."

ANNA FERGUSON

14, high school student

"I wasn't surprised when Erin came out. I think there was already some thought in the back of my mind that she might be gay. At first I didn't think about it very much, but then I started worrying about her physical safety because I had heard about gay bashing. I talked to my mom about it and she said that Erin knew how to take care of herself. I would always tell her to take care of herself. I don't worry so much as I used to, but it's hard not to worry a little.

"I think she's doing really well now. I'll be going to the same high school as Erin did and I think it's a good thing because people really liked her. There's only been one person who's given me a really hard time about it. Sometimes, people say little things like, 'Oh, it's sick,' but I just tell them

it's not. And it's not much harder for me than normal talking but I haven't figured how to answer back some things.

"There was a fencing tournament I had qualified for that was being held when the March on Washington was happening, and I was going to go, but it was in Colorado. I don't know that much about Colorado, except I know that they aren't giving gays and lesbians the same rights that everyone else has. I guess it's not fashionable to not be homophobic there, like it's not fashionable to be racist. So I thought about it for a while, and I decided I just didn't want to go there. When Erin found out, she said, 'Well, why don't you come on the March on Washington with me?' and so I went.

"It was the most fun trip I'd ever had. There were really nice people all around, and at the rally, there were famous people. I like being around gay people. Almost every gay person I've ever met has been really nice to me, except this one guy I met, and I didn't even know he was gay until just a little while ago.

"I made a speech to the Optimists Club. At first I thought I would talk about gay rights in general, but then I decided it would be better if I just talked about Erin. So I talked about how she had a kind of hard time growing up and how in the end she told us, and she became a hero after that. What I really liked was, at the end, when people came up to me and said they were really glad I talked about it because they had a gay relative too. I ended up getting second place, but just between you and me, I think that people liked my speech better.

"Erin is a hero to me. She gets her point across and that's one of the reasons I like her so much. She's so good at that and I've always wanted to be."

Anna, Erin and Rose, Erin's girlfriend, take a stroll in the evening.

NOT FAR FROM THE TREE

BEN ANDERSON'S FAMILY
Olympia, Washington

Ben is the kind of student every college teacher wants: bright, responsible, stimulating. He shows up for class, turns his independent work in on time, collaborates well with other students. He has direction, motivation, and good grades. What he didn't have in 1994 was money. His father had been ill for some time and unable to work; his mom worked but there wasn't enough money for him to be able to continue his undergraduate work. So he applied for a scholarship at The Evergreen State College in Olympia, Washington.

He applied for a minority scholarship. Evergreen is the progressive campus for the Washington State public system, and Ben was not lacking in need, scholastic qualifications or faculty support. But he was still a long-shot for the scholarship because his qualifier for minority status was his sexual orientation.

Ben Anderson is nineteen years old and gay. He comes from a small, conservative, rural town in southwestern Washington, where his parents grew up high school sweethearts. He is polite, as befits his upbringing in a gentle, religious family. But in the spring of 1994, he was ready to stand up and be counted. No one had ever been awarded a minority scholarship on the basis of being gay. That spring, Ben Anderson was the first.

It took a lot off his mind. It made it possible for him to spend more time with his father, who was growing more and more ill due to complications from AIDS. Ben's father is gay, too. His mother continues to shelter the boy-man, and his father from a distance. It seems Ben has not fallen far from either tree.

BEN ANDERSON

19, sophomore college student

"I was named for Benjamin in the Bible, who was one of Joseph's brothers. All three of us kids are named for Biblical people. Both my mother and father are active Catholics. My dad is very devout. My mom is equally religious but she doesn't attend church regularly because of the priest in her town.

"I was raised in that small town, very rural, where all the boys drive those big old Ford pickups with the gun rack and the American flag in the back, and say 'dude' a lot. Both my parents were born there; my grandparents all live there. After my folks got married in their junior year of college, they decided they wanted to raise their family close to the grandparents, to maintain a cohesion of the family. So they moved back.

"I was eleven when they got divorced. They told each kid separately so we had a chance to talk to them one-on-one. I was really pissed and started to cry because it meant my dad was going

Ben Anderson is surrounded by Sarah Anderson, Bob Laster, Ron Anderson and Barbara Anderson.

to not live there. They said he was leaving because he was gay, and it was fine with me because I was pretty sure I was, too. I was mad because they had said they'd never leave each other. I felt betrayed and abandoned.

"I didn't come out until I was sixteen because I didn't want to admit to people that I was gay. Growing up in that town was so horrendous anyway; there wasn't any room for difference. You either fit the mold, or you didn't – and if you didn't, you got hell for it. I didn't accept my gayness because it would have been one more strike against me. I already had a lot of strikes: I was smart; I was completely non-athletic; I was not cool; I was a musician. At school, I knew I should be out playing football instead of role-playing Tolkien. But at home

I was fine. I was clear that the thing that was wrong was out there. It wasn't me.

"When I came out, I didn't want people to think that I was gay because my father was gay. I wanted them to think I'm gay because I am. Maybe there's the whole gene thing, but the main thing he gave me is that he made me feel comfortable being gay. Until I was about seventeen, I did go through a time of not wanting to claim being gay because it just seemed like too much hassle, and too much pain. My dad had gotten fired from a job for being gay, and so it was like, 'Nope.' So I got a girlfriend, and we were pals. It was safety, but I knew I wasn't attracted to her sexually. Every night I prayed for a dream to tell me: yes or no, am I gay? I did finally get a sign. And it was a really cool one.

"My dad got invited to speak to a summer camp in June of 1991. They wanted him to speak as an adult gay man and gay parent. He invited me to go as the straight kid of a gay parent. So I was up there on this panel in front of all these high school kids. I looked at the other kids on the panel and everyone else on the panel was gay and under nineteen. I thought, 'Whoa, if they can do it, I can do it.' It was the first time I'd ever seen other gay kids.

"And that was part of the problem – all the gay folks I knew were adults and pretty stereotypical and I couldn't really see myself in them. But here were all these kids my age, who were so brave, and it was awesome. So I think of that day as the day I came out to myself. Six months later, I came out to my parents.

"When my dad divorced my mom, he moved to a townhouse about five blocks away, and he moved in with his lover, Bob. I was pretty resentful of all the attention Bob got, and sometimes he tried to

act like a parent, but he wasn't yet. I was resentful when he would try to discipline me. It was like, 'Bob, who do you think you are that you would have so much influence?' Now, I think of him as a parent because he does parent things. I'm older now so the power dynamic is more side-to-side than up-and-down. I can talk to him and confront him; he drives me back to school; if I'm totally broke, he'll give me money – that kind of thing.

"There's that whole thing about, 'You can pick your friends but you can't pick your family,' but I really disagree. In my family, it's been a choice. My parents chose to live around my grandparents. I chose to accept Bob as a parental figure. We choose to foster and maintain the bonds that we have.

"I have unconditional support from my family. They give me strength when I think I don't have the strength. My mom is incredibly committed and she does what has to get done. Family people can't really leave – they can try, but they can't really leave you – and you can completely hate them, but you still love them on some obscure level, and you can't leave them either.

After working in the garden, Ron pulls some grass off Barbara.

"Sexuality doesn't really matter. The key isn't that I'm gay and have a gay dad and a straight mom. The key is that I have a mom and dad, a sister and a brother, and a Bob, and they love me, not in spite of, but because of. We accept and embrace each other, and anybody who can't do that has no right calling themselves a family.

"In all likelihood, barring any great miracle, my dad will die of AIDS. And while I wish every day that my life were different, this is the situation I have to deal with. The way I see it, I could spend the rest of my life in misery because of this, or I could choose to learn from the situation and grow, recognizing all my dad teaches me – how to really live, for example. We have choices in how we deal with our lives. My family has chosen to learn from this, and really enjoy the time we have left with each other."

BARBARA ANDERSON
47, special education teacher

"The first time Ron told me he was gay, we'd been married a year and a few months. At that point, neither of us knew a whole lot about it. I didn't want to get divorced unless we were sure he really was gay. So, he saw a psychiatrist in Seattle for several months. Then he came back to me and said that what he really wanted was the marriage to work and to have a family.

"We wondered about Ben from the time he was real little. We thought, very probably, he was gay. And I wanted to have a better response to him than where I was when Ron and I were first married. Because the faith life is important to me, and because I was in grad school taking an ethics class at a Catholic university at the time, I wrote

my term paper on a Catholic's perspective on homosexuality. Ron proofed it for me and his system of denial about his own orientation began to crumble. He came out within the year.

"Jesus never spoke of homosexuality. He spoke very loud and clear on marriage, and yet the Church gives out annulments like they were popcorn. There are a lot of things in the Scripture that the Church does not make any issue over. The things Jesus did talk clearly about were that His Father's house had many rooms, and that the people the world saw as unworthy, who were marginalized and ostracized, were the very ones Jesus went to. It seemed to me we'd be better off erring on the side of compassion and understanding. We are enjoined to be neighbors, so it seemed

to me a more Catholic response to gay humans would be to support gay marriage and gay people and their families, the same way we support other families. I concluded we'd be better off if we recognized God's creativity.

"Since having Ben around as a little guy, there never has been a doubt in my mind about the issue of choice. Ben wasn't choosing to be gay; he was gay. The hard part for me has always been what I knew society would do to him. In fact, I had to watch that happen all along, and my response was to do what I did with all my children: I defended him.

"The worst part now is the way society is going to limit him. I've already seen it and had to be a part of it to try to protect him, like suggesting reconsidering being a teacher. The reality is, right now, he doesn't have near enough protection. The only way he could be a teacher and be gay would be to live in a major city, and even then the danger is huge. A hundred years ago, if a teacher was single and dating, she was kicked out of teaching. Now, it's gay people, and districts find a way to get rid of those people. So I've tried to channel him into other helping professions because that's what he wants to do.

"With Ron, it was very hard. There were the inevitable questions: how could I have been so stupid, that kind of thing. His mother is a staunch fundamentalist Christian who still never talks about it. The divorce was hard on the kids because Ron and I hadn't been fighting and they didn't have any warning. As we shared with friends, and found out some were not friends, the kids saw that and it was tough.

"I wanted to stay friends and family with Ron. He had to be free to live as a gay man, and I needed to be free to live as a straight woman, but our first priority was to protect the kids. In order to keep them healthy through the decision we made, we had to keep as much of the rest of their world, and their support system, as intact as we possibly could. It was never a question of whether or not Ron and I loved each other. It was a question of whether or not we could be married.

"I was mad, but I'm not good at staying mad. I was extremely angry at God for a long time, and

carried on, but then we got on with it. I was angry with Ron because it looked like I was dealing with the emotional baggage of everybody while Ron was off to a new life and very excited about it. But it had nothing really to do with him and me. It had to do with the circumstances – having the kids and I

Ben looks for dirt on his shoe.

stay in the house together, that sort of thing. His life was no bed of roses either, but those were things we fought out.

"He's dying now and I'm taking care of him. The bottom line is, I made vows 25 years ago. The only one I think God nullified is the one about the sexual relationship, not the one about sickness and health, better or worse. I promised to him and to God that I would be there and I meant it. The circumstances have changed, but that hasn't changed.

"I'm blessed that I work for a small district with people who know me, so I have no problem getting off work to take care of him. In an awful lot of circumstances I wouldn't be able to take my sick time to help him, because he's not family since we're divorced. That's a pretty narrow view.

"It's a crock that gay people don't have families. It's pathetic to say that. I get real blunt these days. My last reason for silence is gone. I feel very sorry for people who are so uninformed and bigoted. Every time we have an election, it bugs the hell out of me to hear these Christian sorts pointing to gays as the reason for the decline in family values.

"A lot of these 'wonderful' Christian families kick out a kid and have him suicide because there's something about that kid they don't approve of. They're so busy being right, they have no idea what their kids are about. I think those are sick families.

"It makes me really mad to have our family dismissed because there are some people in our family who are gay and some who are straight; some who are black and some who are white; some who are old and some who are young; we have some disabled, some not. Okay, so our tapestry has more colors than some others. If they choose to live with gray, it's okay, I guess, if that's

their idea of pretty. But it's not ours."

RON ANDERSON

47, retired credit union administrator

"Ben and I have always been extremely close. When Ben was two, I knew he was gay. We were at the beach, and maybe because he was so sensitive, I can't remember how I knew, but it crossed my mind. Nothing after that surprised me. When he finally came out, I felt like perhaps I hadn't made such a mess. I felt good for him, that he was able to be so open. There was a time when Ben didn't feel so good about me being gay. We discussed how it was for him to talk about his own gayness and suddenly mine made more sense to him."

BOB LASTER

45, teacher and director of cosmetology school

"Being part of this family is really good for me. It gives me an obligation and a purpose. That's why I'm around. My name isn't going down in history, but I'm making my mark with this family. When I obligated myself to the situation, I knew that even if Ron and I broke up, which we did, I was still going to be obligated to the family unit. This was something I didn't want to be wishy-washy about.

"I want the kids to always see Ron and me together, the same way they see their mom with Ron. I think this will give them some solid ground, to know that there's something good in everything.

"My family is interracial and I was brought up in an environment where I saw different colors and different cultures. The neighborhood took care of all of us. When we went to the back door, they knew who we were. You either ate there or you didn't, but

they knew where you did eat. It was a tribal family unit. So I've always known you could create family through love and not have to have the blood."

SARAH ANDERSON

14, middle school student

"Ben told me he was gay when he was a junior in high school. At first I thought he was joking, but he seemed real serious. I didn't really mind, because it didn't make him any different. I was in kindergarten when I knew about my dad. I was sad because it meant my dad had to move out. It didn't bother me that he was gay because he was still my dad. He was just my dad in a different house.

"Most people know about my dad. Nobody treats me in any different way. I think if some kids knew they'd give me a hard time. But I wouldn't really mind, because those people are the real jerks and not my friends, anyway.

"I think it's cool. It makes our family different and I think that's good. Otherwise it would be like going to another person and saying, 'Oh, my family's just like any other family.' You get to tell them something different and I think that's kind of neat.

"Ben and I fight a lot, stupid brother and sister things, but I love him a lot.

"I think a family is someone you can't get rid of. There's a whole bunch of people who would come to you if you needed them, and even if you don't want them there, they won't leave. And it's a good feeling. It makes me feel loved."

[Ron Anderson died on March 11, 1995 at 2:00 a.m. surrounded by family. He was calm, at peace, and without pain.]

On a climb to clear out the cobwebs, Ben reaches a vista overlooking the Columbia River gorge.

SATURDAY IN THE SUBURBS

DUC HONG TA AND SCOT WEGNER'S FAMILY

Palmdale, California

Not all of us gay folk live in big city gay ghettos. Most of us live where everyone else lives, spread out over the rest of America. We hold jobs, pay taxes, mow the yard, just like everyone else. The house of Scot Wegner and Duc Hong Ta is immaculate with three bedrooms, huge kitchen and breakfast nook, formal dining room, formal living room with a black leather sofa and scarlet pillows, den with a big screen television, and a patio with a picnic table in the back yard.

On the day we came to town, every inch of it was full of people. It was a football Saturday. The USC and WSU fans were in the den cheering. There were babies underfoot, and the dining room table was crammed with food for all. There were folks on the patio and children in the yard– women and men gossiping and laughing. But for a football Saturday, it wasn't wild, and it wasn't loud, and I didn't see anyone drinking. One by one, family members came back to me as I sat in the bedroom that was used as a library, and each told me they had made an effort to be there because Duc and Scot had said it was a family day. There were so many people, so many heartfelt stories, I interviewed people for a full eight hours. When I finally emerged, the football game was over but now they were playing a word game, still happy with each other, still laughing. There were no

fights. No one got beat up after the game or went home angry. It was a swell party and one to which I was pleased to have been invited. Who wouldn't like to have these guys as neighbors?

DUC HONG TA

34, law library assistant

"I was born in Vietnam and lived there until I was 14. I left just before the fall of South Vietnam in April of 1975. My oldest sister was married to an American soldier, who later worked for a civilian company. They knew when the country was falling so they were able to make arrangements to get us out.

"When they told me I thought, 'Going to America? This is something only happening in a dream.' We had two hours to get ready. My brother-in-law took us to his company and we hid in his office until we could board the ship. I have three sisters, two in America and one who stayed in Vietnam. I have two brothers. One finally made it over here after about six or seven attempts to flee. The other is still in Vietnam. My mother died two years before I left, and my father chose to stay. He said he wanted to die where he was born, but he wanted us to go – we still had our futures ahead of us. But I'm a strong survivor. I missed my father terribly when he died. I couldn't return to Vietnam

to attend his funeral.

"The first few years here were hard; I couldn't understand anything. We went to Nome, Alaska first. It was one climate extreme to another.

"About being gay – I knew there was something in me when I was seven or eight, but I didn't know what it was. And I didn't know it was so powerful as to overtake me. I was able to move along with the other guys at school, but finally, when I was in high school in America, I had some strange feelings about looking at Caucasian men. I couldn't understand, you know, the hairy legs. I thought there was something wrong with me. I decided to see what was going on, so in college I took a class in human sexuality.

I was afraid to talk to my family members. Homosexuality is a big taboo in Vietnamese culture, the biggest disgrace that could ever happen to one family. Of course, it's there, but it's very suppressed. Sex in general in Vietnam is not widely discussed. What I've learned from older gay Vietnamese men here in America is that there was only one place in all of Saigon to meet other gay men. Thailand is very free; it's totally different. But in Vietnam, you don't tell anyone. In Vietnam, you may be gay, but you get married anyway.

"In college, I felt I was the only one who was Oriental and gay. So I moved to Los Angeles

Left to right, back row: Mike Carr, Harry Presser, Roger Wong, Danny Guido, Linda Burns, Ray Tokomoto, Joe Erne...
Scot Holland, Dina Holland, Anna Gee. Front row: Connie Saldin, John Saldin, Lindsey Saldin, Siena Holla...
Duc Hong Ta, Scot Wagner, Brenda Stallings, Urbain Lausier. Foreground, Stacy Saldi...

A televised football game fills time on a Fall Saturday. Duc, left, watches his alma mater, WSU, go down to defeat against USC. Ray, with pom poms, is a USC fan.

because there were more gay men here, and more Asians too. Scot was dating a good friend of mine. Things didn't work out for him, and things didn't work out in my relationship either, so in 1991, we decided to give it a try.

"I found out Scot's a very caring guy, very loving and understanding. We have been giving it the best of what we've got, and have tried to stay on the same path. We talk about what we want to do as a couple, and how we'll achieve the goals of staying together and have something for ourselves that we can call ours. I am proud of our relationship. I feel strongly that I'm married to Scot.

"We have rings and one earring each which match. It was a very daring thing to get my ear

pierced. My workplace is very conservative. I don't bring in my personal life.

"I just came out to my family seven months ago. My older sister said it didn't matter who I was with, as long as I was happy. One sister asked me if I was trying to shame the family, but I explained that wasn't it, and that if she asked me to change I couldn't. It would be like asking me to cut off my right hand. I'm just giving her more time to get used to it. My brother said he would not interfere with what I considered happiness. I felt good about coming out.

"I'm a Buddhist by birth and in my heart, and the Buddha never said anything about homosexuality. It's not like the Bible.

"The Vietnamese way of life is that if you don't have your own family members with you, those who are close around you are now your family. When I don't feel like my friends are straight, for example – when there's no division – then we've crossed the barrier into family."

SCOT WEGNER

34, management, software design development

"Duc is my life partner. I see us as married. I've been in several long relationships, but this is the first time I ever considered getting a ring. It was a

big turning point in my life. I've always been against the idea of rings because the world in general treats you differently if they see a ring on your wedding finger. There were certain expectations that were weird to me. But with Duc and me, it's a natural thing.

"I grew up in Kirkland, Washington. My family is of German-Swiss heritage. Part of the reason I came to Southern California to go to school was because I didn't really know how to come out in Washington.

"When I came out to my parents, it wasn't marvelous. My step-mom was fine; she's from Pasadena. My father took it a little more personally. After six months when he didn't talk to me, things got a lot better. Now he asks about Duc, and we went up for Thanksgiving, and they're nice to him.

"At an Asian dance club Duc and I met when we were both breaking up with our boyfriends. We just talked, week after week. Finally we set up a date to see a Lakers play-off game on television. Because we

Dina Holland, Scot Holland, Scot Wegner, and Linda Burns chat in the backyard over dinner.

were just coming out of relationships, we both wanted to go slow. He was just ending a seven-year relationship. He wanted to make sure if he had another relationship, it was the right one. And I had things to clean up in my life. So it was quite a while before we moved in together, at least a year.

"We've moved into a real suburban community here but the people have accepted us and have been wonderful. And that's one thing I want America to do, to accept us as neighbors, because that's who we are. None of the people here today hesitated when I asked them to come to be part of this. It means a lot to me."

BRENDA STALLINGS
44, legal secretary

"Duc and I are a lot alike; we're both Leos and our personalities click. He's a very personable person. We spend up to four hours a day in the car driving into work. We like the same kind of music and that helps! We both like 70's disco. I'm a real dancer, and the only clubs where you can go and dance and not worry about somebody hitting on you are the gay clubs, so Duc and I have that in common, too.

"In Black culture, if you're from the South, you're more apt to be family oriented, more likely to spend time together. People born in the city, on the East Coast, once the kids come of age, the family separates. They aren't as close knit as they should be. You find in Black culture we don't always stay as close together as we should and we don't get as much accomplished as we could. There have been times when my blood family didn't help me when I needed help, but in my social family, there's always someone there in my corner, who will help through thick and thin."

Duc, with Scot's god daughter, Siena Holland.

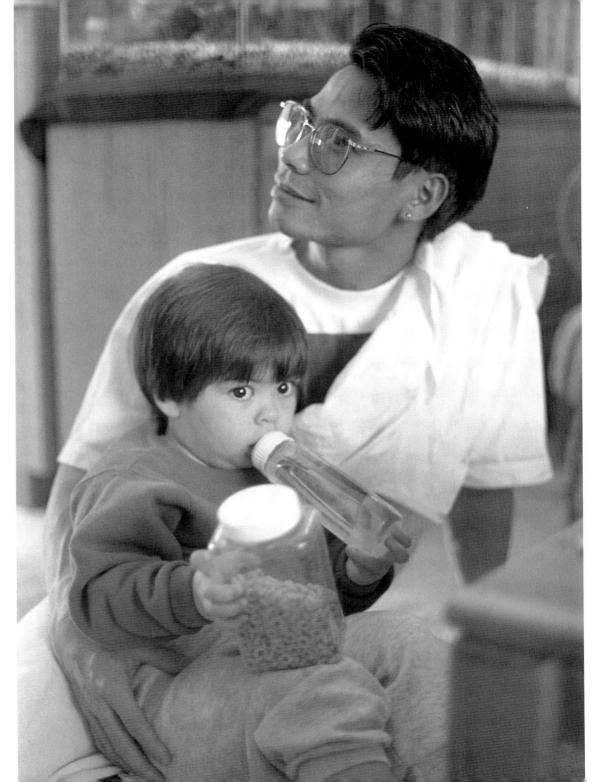

Duc wears a tee shirt with a map of Vietnam, his home country.

MICHAEL CARR

38, software engineer

"I've worked with Scot for about five years now, and I found out he was gay about two days after I got there. In many ways, I'm closer to Scot than I am to my own sister.

"I think gay people should be allowed to be married. Who doesn't want that sense of belonging that you get in a family? When the Torah was written, 5,000 years ago, they had certain laws, and maybe it was right to abide by those laws then. But fundamentally, people change. Why shouldn't the laws?"

DINA HOLLAND

33, personnel agency

"Scot is Siena's godfather. We knew that for the longest time Scot wanted a child. He was really happy for us when we were pregnant. I trust him to care for my child. In a crunch, I would trust him to raise my child. And he's willing to do it."

RAY TOKUMOTO

32, travel agent

"I know, if I were having difficulties with Joe, I could call Scot up and discuss very personal and confidential things. And I would do the same for him. I am getting older, and I can take care of people too, now."

In a game called Taboo, the object is to get your team to guess a word, without using certain forbidden words.

Duc and Scot both play on a gay men's soccer team in Los Angeles.

SUNDAY AT HOME

PAT AND CHERRY HUSSAIN · SPENCER AND NIKKI WILLIAMS
Atlanta, Georgia

The garden in their suburban Atlanta home needs work and Cherry frets over it. Pat has promised to help, one of these days. It's not that Cherry worries about what the neighbors think – far from it. It's that she likes to work in the earth, always has; she's a farm girl, she says. She would like to get at it, maybe today, since everybody's home.

Or maybe not today. Because everybody is home. Maybe today, they'll all just hang out together – or maybe they'll play that balancing game, Jenga, all of them carefully negotiating the terrain of their lives, the teenagers and Pat and her. They will move the dining room table into the living room, so there is enough space for everyone to pace around it, to get a good angle, each taking their own play, in their own style, in their own good time, while shouting down the others. Cherry likes to win; usually she does. But anything could happen today because everybody's home.

The car rusting in the front yard is Spencer's, and Cherry frets about that too. If the boy can't take care of it, he can't drive it. Very simple. She'd show him how to fix it if he'd ask. Well, he'll get tired of needing the car soon enough. When she comes over Nikki takes the bus. Both kids used to live with their father; then one day, two years ago, Spencer called from school and said, 'Come and get me,' and so they did. Got a court order so he

could stay. But Nikki has stayed with her father, to take care of him, the girl says.

After she left their father, the children were taken from Cherry because she was a lesbian. And so with Pat standing by her, making sure her ex-husband never hits her again, Cherry has waited for her children to come home. Today, they will have the whole day. Maybe the hard lessons they've learned about how to be close without always living together can be put to use today in this family garden she refuses to let go to seed.

CHERRY HUSSAIN

39, stockperson in a grocery store

"My whole family knows I'm a bulldyke. My husband was abusing me before I was gay and it got worse after I came out to him, but he's been a jerk from the beginning, so I don't think it was any reason, it was just an excuse.

"I raised my children to be non-judgmental, not to make fun of someone's difference, and if you have a problem, always talk to me about it. Like all parents, I worry about peer pressure on my son and daughter; I worry about trying to ease that for them. But kids are honest and cruel, and there's nothing I can do to stop that. All I can do is to try to prepare them for taunting and teasing. I've always been open with them so someone can't come and tell

them something they don't know. I was brought up to tell the truth and stick to it. And I want my children to be 98 years old and still have it be the way it is now: I want them to be able to talk to me about anything. I just want their minds open.

"My plan is to be here with Pat the rest of my life. Where can I start to tell you about the best thing about my relationship with Pat? The best part is knowing that I'm loved 24 hours of the day, seven days a week, 365 days a year. It's not, 'I love you,' for five minutes and 'hate you' for the next ten.

"Pat loves me – how can I explain it? I can describe it. It's like being surrounded by a cocoon. That cocoon is surrounded by all the things it needs to nurture and mold itself into this beautiful butterfly. Pat loves me with her whole self, and not just a part of it. I get 125% of it and sometimes more. I light up when I think about it. When I'm not around her, I miss her. That's love to me.

"Families pick you up when the ground jumps up and knocks you down, and support you, push you and encourage you. Why should we have to talk about gay and lesbian families? Why can't it just be family? We were all created by a much higher, supreme being, and whatever created us made us all out of love. We're getting a test. I think we haven't figured it out yet."

Left to right, Spencer Williams, Pat Hussain, Cherry Hussain, and Nikki William.

This Atlanta family plays a very competitive version of Jenga, a balancing game.

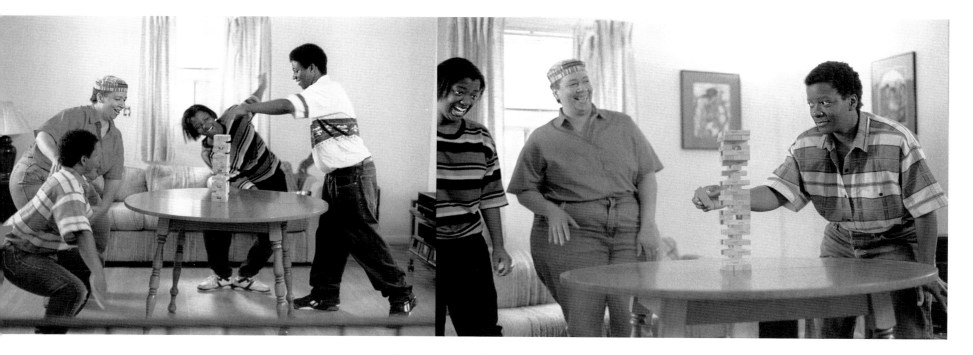

PAT HUSSAIN

44, lesbian and gay anti-racist freedom organizer

"Cherry and I have been together for nine years. We were married in 1990. I live now with her son and I think of him, and Cherry's daughter, as also my son and my daughter.

"The theory that women become lesbian or bisexual because of bad experiences with men just falls apart when it comes to me, and even if that were true, if abuse by men made women lesbians, there would be very few heterosexual women left in this country. My father is a wonderful man, did lots of interesting things. My mom was a reading specialist and I was reading at age three.

"I came out late. I was 28. All of my family was supportive. The reaction mostly was, 'You're not sick? We can deal with a dyke daughter; we just want to make sure you don't have some illness.' But the culture in which I was raised speaks to a group of people who have had to struggle for survival from when the first ships were loaded to bring us here chained in their bellies. The thought is that if you are not procreating, somehow you are not doing your part to help the race carry on. I think that's just a modification of what's coming from the white community – we don't procreate, therefore, there's no reason for us to have any type of committed relationship. How that plays out, is that men who've had vasectomies or women

who've had hysterectomies are not allowed to marry, and that marriage licenses are issued on a conditional basis – you have a certain amount of time to have children before your marriage license is revoked. But of course, this is not what happens. It's just a smoke-and-mirror weapon that's being used against us.

"The age-old ploy to rid any society, in particular this one, of people who the powers that be have decided they don't want around, has three parts. The first part is to dehumanize that group to make them not like yourself – for example, they don't procreate or, for example, gay and lesbian people don't have families. Once you've dehumanized someone, set them apart and given them a different set of characteristics, then you play up those differences and turn them into demonic things. You put the horns and the tail on them – they are child molesters, recruiters of children, they have no way to increase their ranks other than taking your daughter or your son. The demonization plays on fear, much more than the dehumanization process, which is more rational. Then it's okay, in any society, to destroy the demon.

"That is what I believe some of those who call themselves the right wing, who I call Salemites, are doing. Salemites is my word for those people because they are neither religious, nor are they right. They are the people who were behind the religious hysteria of the Salem witch trials, who allowed people to be killed and imprisoned while they were waving the cross. This hysteria is not a new thing in this country. It has played itself out around slavery and racism. I'm really tired of the shorthand name KKK; they are the Christian Knights of the Ku Klux Klan and their symbol is a cross. We have seen what that type of religious hysteria does.

"When desegregation became the law here in Atlanta, there were ministers saying, 'We will not submit to the immoral Supreme Court, we will continue to follow God's law, and God has ordained this separation of the races. Integration is an abomination.' These people thought they were right through Biblical study. In the '60s, they said integration was not about equal rights. It was about race-mixing and getting white women for black men. Sometimes I feel like I'm in a time warp. The country has amnesia on the moral aspect, on the sexual aspect, and on the religion aspect of these issues. When I look at the same type of religious

fervor, the same chill runs through my body.

"The best thing about my family is being able to laugh and talk. There's not really anything off limits here. If it's on your mind, say it. Sometimes I think there's just not enough laughter in the world, and these people do make me laugh. Like playing Jenga. I didn't even want to play that game. I knew I could not win this game in a million years. I have never won. But Cherry talked me into it and I did win. They kept talking at me, and talking trash, and it helps me to laugh at myself.

"I'm going to be with this woman forever. She's the best thing that ever happened to me. She's made me slow down. My family never hugged or touched. Cherry's changed all that. She's taught me to relax. We go fishing. My objective is to catch the fish – *wrong*. We're there to just hang out. She slowed me down to where I could realize there's a whole other world.

"Love is so hard to have, so fragile and yet can be so resilient, why would anyone want to crush it? Why would you want to do anything else but create more love in the world?"

EUGENIA 'NIKKI' WILLIAMS

15, high school student

"I live with my dad, a couple of miles from here. I come over on the bus when I want to come over. I don't really remember how old I was when my mom left.

"I like Pat. She's nice. She's funny. She's in my family, sort of. I mean, I don't see her and my mom as married, but they do live together. My family is fun – it's people to talk to. I talk to my mom about everything, anything. I don't hardly see my dad. He's usually off working or taking pictures. But I love him. I'm close to Spencer but we hardly ever see each other unless I come over here.

"I hear kids at school making fun of lesbians, but I don't care. It used to bother me, but I got older. I just ignore it.

"I see Pat on television all the time, for all her activism, and it makes me feel like I know a celebrity. I'm proud of her, but she doesn't like seeing herself on TV. It worries her that somebody might want to hurt her because they might not be agreeing with what she's saying, so she won't even watch. But I don't think anybody would do that. If they did, they'd have me looking for them, and Spencer and the police and everybody. They wouldn't get too far."

SPENCER WILLIAMS

16, high school student

"I was around ten or nine when my mom left. At the time, I thought she was coming back. Me and my sister, we were upset, but after a while we got used to it. I stayed with my dad, and we got along all right, but sometimes I got real mad, because I had to go to a school I didn't want to go to, and he always got on my case about stuff, so I just left.

"Here, it's better. I'm going to a better school and I'm doing better in my classes and I have a little more freedom, like that.

"I know my mom's gay. It bothers me but I don't let it bother me. Like when she first met Pat, it bothered me a lot. I didn't want to have anything to do with them. But after awhile, I just let it go. I don't know really what about it bothers me. One of these days, I'm going to figure it out, but until then, I just don't know.

"At school, nobody knows I live with Pat. Kids do make fun of gay people, but folks are going to do what they are going to do and you just have to learn to live with a lot of stuff.

"Family to me is a group of folk who are together, work together, have fun together. Cherry's my family, and my sister and my dad. I got one mom and that's how many I want. Pat can be cool. We have our differences – she is a friend to me, though. You can have a family and nobody cares about anybody, and just go on about their business, but a family should be more like everybody's tight with each other. And I have that, pretty much. Sometimes, I get pretty mad, myself, but we get back on track with each other."

EVERY DAY PRAYERS

KEVIN SANCHEZ'S FAMILY
San Francisco, California

Everyone seemed to have a different story about Kevin Sanchez. A wild man, tattoo on the side of his head. A gentle man in recovery. Motorcycles and leather. Committed long-term partnership. One of the dancers from the dance. Native American spiritual with a laugh bright as dawn. So many stories.

They were all true. Kevin Sanchez grew up in Martinez, California in that post-war booming delta land near San Francisco. His father is a quiet Latino man with a Ute tribal affiliation, a man who worked hard with his hands all his life, a family man who folds his hands as if in prayer and then twists them anxiously apart to grasp a can of beer when asked about his son's health. His mother is Anglo, laughs in spite of herself when Kevin reminds her about their wild escapades in discos in the City years ago. She is tight with her family, and Kevin grew up in a house two doors down from his grandmother and his aunts who have always seemed more like his sisters.

Two years ago, Kevin buried Scott, his partner of ten years. He was four months sober at the time. He actively cultivates family these days, even though the hurt from Scott's death still cuts so deep, he knows he'll never be able to tell Brian, the man who loves him now, exactly how much he means to him. It is not an easy time; he is often

sick. Most of his old friends are gone. Like the rest of us, he fantasizes about having money but what he'd do is different: he'd buy three condos in the expensive high-rise up the street from the apartment where he now lives in San Francisco's Tenderloin – one for his aunt Dorothy, one for his aunt Dianna and one for him, in the middle. He knows he won't live that long. But now that he knows he deserves it, he is making his family strong before he goes.

KEVIN SANCHEZ
35, barber

"I hold licenses for both barbering and cosmetology. The difference between the two is mainly political. Barbering is a lost art, but my lesbian aunt was a barber and we worked together in the men's barber shops. My aunt is a babe; no one knew she was a dyke. She was the first woman barber in Contra Costa County, and was harassed, called a whore and got a lot of bad press. But I'm proud of her.

"I have two brothers, and I have an extended family of two hundred people (at the last family reunion). Who was around when I was young was: my aunt Dorothy, who is only seven years older than me and who had an extensive Barbie collection (including the car); my mom's mother who

Kevin Sanchez races around San Francisco's Twin Peaks on his motorcycle.

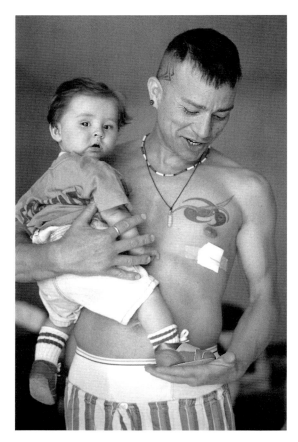

Kevin holds Thomas Jelen. The patch on his chest is a catheter for administering medication

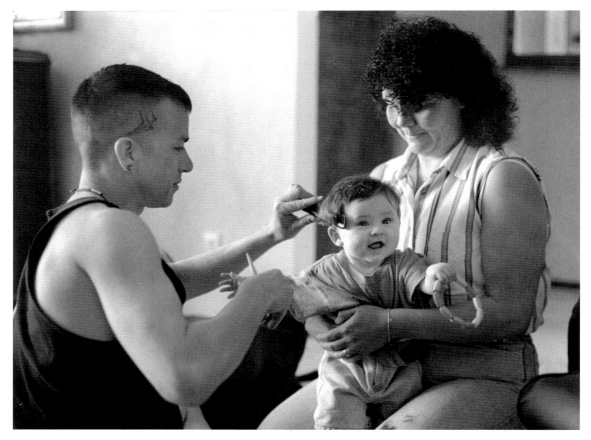

Pat Jelen holds her son while Kevin gives him his first haircut.

lived two doors down; and my aunt Dianna, the barber. I didn't have a lot to do with my father's family, largely I think because my mother was fearful of things that were not familiar to her. My father was very there with us; our weekends were always about hunting, skiing, motorcycles, that sort of thing. I realized recently that I've always worn

boots; even when I'm wearing a dress I have to wear boots! Last week, I looked down and I saw my father's feet.

"I worked in gay barber shops in San Francisco and they were pretty sexually oriented, but the straight ones were too, lots of porno, that kind of thing. I worked at the Male Image on Market

Street for years. In 1980, we dressed up like the Village People and I was the Army Private in the boots, but if we were to do it now, I'd be the Indian. No one did the Indian. I was kind of embarrassed by my heritage then. But I'm only one of two who are left from the original crew. The other guy is HIV negative; everybody else is dead.

Del Oplinger, Kevin's sponsor in Narcotics Anonymous, reflects on their friendship

I've had full-blown AIDS for more than a year now and have been HIV positive for nine.

"Scott, my partner of ten years, died September 25 two years ago. Everything in my life is marked by that event, before and after. I don't think about time much; I just keep noticing I'm still here. He was very stable and predictable. I was always enough for him and he didn't want much else outside of our home. I resisted that; I wanted more.

"We were both from Martinez. He was from the Catholic school crowd, so we didn't really hang with each other. My crowd was trash, the public school trash. I was 24 when I met him. He was 19, a real baby. I brought him out. I was jaded already; I'd been involved in a heavy sex and drug scene in the City before I was 18. I was on Polk Street at 15 and I'd been around the block. As a third generation addict, it was kind of acceptable behavior. But I was his first and only lover, and that carries a lot of heavy stuff for me.

"My parents' home was kind of the Lost Boys Home. All the boys who didn't have fathers loved my father and hung around at my house. There's an extended family that's still there. But because

I've been through so much in the last few years, I don't operate much like my family any more. They are unconscious a lot of the time and I don't live that way anymore, having AIDS, being in recovery, being a gay male, identifying as an American Indian (since my mother is white, I didn't really have permission to do that at home). But my family is very, very loving and I love them too.

"For years, I was told that I didn't have a claim to God because I was a homosexual, and I finally allowed myself to have that claim. I can create my own belief in God, and I can create my own family by claiming them. I can sense when someone wants me to be happy, joyous and free, and that intention, that love, is like claiming me back.

"So I am claiming all of my family. I realized that I had never gone out with my brothers, not even once. I chose to go away. No one ever told me to go off, but I felt unclaimed as a gay person. I bought into that myth that there was something wrong with me. I remember when I was about eight, my mom told me about my aunt Dianna. It was all very hushed and the energy behind it was sad and scared.

"My aunt Dianna was an active addict, suicidal, and institutionalized for being lesbian. By coincidence, I had just read in the dictionary about homosexuals and I knew immediately that's what I was. So I had a suicide plan, even at that age. I

knew that society would think I was sick and possibly would even try to hurt or kill me, and I also had this feeling I would never be happy. I remember thinking I can probably hide this until I'm about sixteen and then, I thought, I would just kill myself.

"It did help me to have a lesbian aunt. She was very loving, and she had a home. Uncle Marilyn lived there with her, and she was pretty fabulous with her motorcycle and everything. But for a long time, I thought that gay meant using drugs and for a while there, I thought AIDS meant a

Dorothy Bickert, an aunt since she was seven, says she feels more like Kevin's sister.

great excuse for being totally ripped. I haven't found a comfortable way to tell people I'm in recovery now because I'm afraid I'll be judged, and I am. People who aren't addicts don't understand, and people who are addicts who aren't ready to stop yet don't understand.

"I called Del the day after Scott died because I knew he had survived something I was going through. He has really helped me, being in recovery himself. I didn't have a lot of guidance when I was growing up. But Del gently calls me on stuff, and I trust that he'll never manipulate me for his own gain. I think he's willing to have pain, even, to help me. That's one of the ways I know he's family. I know he's not going to attack me – he's going to support me – and I can't say that about some of my blood family.

"As I get sicker, and can't physically control

things anymore, my role in the world and in my family is changing. I've noticed that the last couple of times I've called my parents and asked them to come down, they have, which is new for them. I guess I'm really unsure about what's happening and it's scary. I've never not done for myself. I can't hide it anymore and it's getting more uncomfortable with everybody. I feel more removed from life than I ever have.

"Brian, my boyfriend, is the one I call these days for support. I miss him when he's not around. He

makes me laugh. We have a level of trust and comfort that I haven't had with anyone else. But ever since Scott died, I've had a problem committing to anything. I'm afraid. I think I'm probably more in love with Brian than I will ever let him know. My natural reaction is to just run and be by myself, but I haven't. I can't get high anymore, and some days I can't even get out of bed! I'm not done yet, whatever that means, but it's getting harder and harder to be here. I think it's going to be a push to be here when this book comes out."

DIANNA MATTHEWS

55, barber

"During Kevin's formative years, I lived in the City, but I've been close to him all his life. When he was nine or ten, I was in a long-term relationship with a woman named Marilyn who he really loved. She was a little on the butch side. She had tattoos and always rolled her sleeves up and Kevin called her Uncle Marilyn. She stayed in our lives too, after we split up; she'd always come back and check up on the kids and visit. When we broke up, it was very hard on the family. It was harder on my father than it was on me! I'd come out to my family in the 1950's and they totally accepted me from the get-go.

"Kevin got sober before I did, but now, it's brought us much closer together. Before we always got along, but it was hard to connect. I'm glad we're both getting ourselves together now, especially because of the position he's in. Going through this with him, not hiding behind alcohol and drugs anymore – it's really scary because I love him so much. I'm scared to see him hurting."

LEVI SANCHEZ

56, retired carpenter

"At first when I found out about Kevin being gay, it was uncomfortable, him not being the same, but as it went on, you get used to it. Now, the way I look at it, if Kevin's happy, I'm happy.

"Scott was my son's friend and lover and he was one great kid. I loved him. He was like my own son and it was a terrible loss. My kid's got a little of the rebel in him and Scott was more like me, kind of laid back. I'm worried about Kevin now, and I hope he can get a handle on this AIDS thing. We're praying that there will be a cure for it. I'm not going to give up on him. If there was anything I could do, I'd do it. If and when it happens, I'm going to be devastated. But I'm not going to let it bother me now.

"I'm a Catholic, but I don't pay much attention to what they say about gay people. I go to church but I have my own belief and I go by that. I pray every day. All I wish is that they'd come up with a cure."

MATT GARRIGAN

41, minister

"Being part of Kevin's family feels like being home. It's like there is an unseen lineage because we aren't biological family, but we certainly are connected. We're connected on a spiritual level, for sure. It feels like I've known him before. I can look at his face and know when he's going to laugh. When he laughs, I feel like I'm at home. When I look at his face, I experience the same thing I do when I look at my biological brothers and they laugh.

"Family feels eternal; there is no exile. For me,

Left to right on the roof of Kevin's apartment: Matt Garrigan, Calvin Perkins, Dianna Matthews, Pat Jelen, Levi Sanchez, Barbara Sanchez, Ray Sanchez, Kevin Sanchez, and Thomas Jele

Aunt Dianna sadly contemplates the prospect of losing her nephew to AIDS.

family sits with God, so there is no such thing as outside it. You can't be banished from it. It's something I can draw on and I can feel it everywhere. The gay men and lesbians I know are so willing to extend the gift of family. We get to choose to be in the family, and that's very powerful. We had to take care of ourselves when no one else would. And it's pretty easy for us to get down to the truth because we lived so long in hiding, we can see it pretty well. That's a great gift to bring because many people are hiding in their own families, afraid to come out with their real feelings. Gay and lesbian families have a lot to offer; when someone begins to tell the truth about themselves, the whole family begins to heal.

"There is no monopoly on Christ. No sect has a monopoly on who He is. Anything that has to do with damnation or guilt is just manipulating Christ. When that Word gets used to exclude someone, I believe somebody is coming from fear and they have to manipulate the Word to make themselves feel safer. We were created in the image and likeness of God, and to think that we have changed that is pretty arrogant."

BRIAN SMITH

29, former waiter, now disabled with HIV

"I found out when I was 21 that I was HIV positive, and the circumstances of finding out were hard. I'd run away from home because of my sexuality and had been living out here for a few years, sort of a wild life. I decided I would go back to Pennsylvania and join the Army because it was a dream of my father's for one of us kids to go into the service, and none of my older brothers would do it. I felt like I had seen a lot in my travels in those three years and got burnt out really fast. I thought going into the Army might be a way to change my life. Five days before I was supposed to go to basic training, the Army told me I was positive. It was devastating. My father told me I knew what I had to do, and that was that I couldn't stay there, because of the repercussions on

them. So I came back here.

"I wasn't surprised when he said that. I talk to them now, but we don't talk about the HIV — although my mother did say that she would rather have her son be gay than be a junkie. They've been very supportive about me getting clean and sober. I've been clean and sober for about fourteen months now. I was going to die a junkie so my parents would never know. At least, with my sobriety, I'll be able to die with a little dignity even though they've abandoned me.

"The first time I saw Kevin, I knew I was going to love him. He's the first person in all my life that I've felt something about. He's very strong; he really looks AIDS right in the face. I feel very lucky to be in his life. I have a commitment to myself that I will stand by him to the end. I've also made a promise to myself that I won't use when he goes, that I won't pick it up just because of my pain. He'll still be around me after he dies.

"Last night, I was comforting him because he was scared. I knew what he was scared of. We cuddle up a lot together; he cuddles underneath my chin and puts his head on my chest and falls asleep. That's when I'm the happiest, and it's when I feel the safest, and it's when I know that two men sharing a bed is a truly beautiful thing."

Father and son share a hug.

"...it's when I know that two men sharing a bed is a truly beautiful thing." – Brian Smith

COMING TO AMERICA

VICTOR GAITAN AND ROBERTO GARCIA'S FAMILY
Alameda, California

Victor Gaitan's brother bought part of his freedom for him by paying a coyote, a guide to illegal immigrants, $300 to lead him across the U.S.-Mexican border, but it was Victor, young, strong, smart and full of heart, who seized his future and pounded it out in hard desert as he ran all night for his life. Like his father before him, he has worked at menial jobs U.S. citizens didn't want. But now, established and respectable, he works as an AIDS counselor for Latino clients. He pays his taxes. He makes a contribution to his community. He is in a strong partnership with another Latino man, Roberto Garcia, from Brownsville, Texas.

Here, Victor is not persecuted as much for being gay. And while there is racism, and painful exclusion, he has found a new family from which he gathers strength. He remains close to his mother and his sisters in Mexico; he is a devoted son, dreaming of bringing his mother to the U.S., where he can care for her until she dies. Roberto is close to Victor's mother, and Victor has become part of Roberto's extended family, too. They are good men, strong men, loving men. The U.S. is lucky to have them.

VICTOR GAITAN

27, AIDS counselor

"I was born in San Miguel, De Allende, Mexico. We were poor people; there isn't a lot of middle class in Mexico – there are rich people and poor people. My father was a bracero; he was one of those men who came to California, Texas and Florida in different seasons to pick. My father was not much at home. I grew up mostly with my brothers and sisters and my mother.

"I came to America the first time in 1980 with my mother. I was around twelve years old. We stayed in Dallas for eight months, but I didn't like it so I went back to Mexico. My mother and father stayed in Texas until 1982 because they needed to work. I lived with my father's mother in Mexico. In 1986, I decided to try to come again.

"A big reason I came to America was because I am gay. I had hope for a better life. I crossed the border because I didn't have papers. It was scary and difficult, and very shameful to have to cross a frontier in order to survive. My brother bought my freedom. I came with a coyote; we crossed at night. I ran from 9 p.m. to 6 a.m. through the desert.

"I didn't know if my mother knew I was gay, but she heard the gossip. She would say, 'I prefer my sons to be gay than to be robbers or assassins,'

when she talked with the comadres, the ladies around. She gave me a hint that no matter what I was, I was going to be welcome in her heart. I am in touch with her now and she loves me very much. She encouraged me to be in a relationship and to be safe. She loves Roberto and calls him her friend. And that's very unusual for a 70 year-old lady who grew up with all the prejudice about homosexuality. I have an older brother who is gay and who lives here in Berkeley but my father kicked him out when he caught him having sex. My brother is very bitter and hates the family. Because my mother didn't want to repeat what had happened with him, and because of my relationship with my mother, she accepted me very easily. And he really resented that. So we don't talk anymore. It's been very ugly and sad.

"I'll always love my brother, but Roberto is my only family here. I knew I could have sex with a man and enjoy it, but I didn't know I could love a man and feel his heart until I had this relationship. We are sharing our lives – we are growing up as human beings. Roberto and I have our problems like anybody else, but I have a commitment to him: to be with him, to respect him, to be loyal, to be truthful, and to love him. I would love to be married in a church. I want my family to be in on it. I want my wedding to be like any other wed-

Left to right, on the beach in Alameda, California: Carlos Lopez, Roberto Garcia, Victor Gaitan, Olivia Gomez, Jorge Gom Carmen Garcia Lopez, Marco Antonio Lopez, Anthony Lopez, Adriana Lopez, and Sergio Lop

Victor plays with Carlitos, his sister-in-law's son.

ding: I want to get dressed up and have lots of flowers and I want all my sisters and brothers and my mother to be there. Part of what is stopping me is that my family can't come to this country. I'm going to become a citizen next year and within six months I can bring my mother here. I will take care of her until she dies.

"Roberto's family has accepted me. I get along well with his sister's family. They respect me. In the Latino society, you love your friends as your family.

I have a friend I love as my brother. Joel and I have been through a lot here in the United States. He came the same way I did. We met, we shared lots of cold winters, we were both busboys in the same restaurant. Joel could come to my house with his luggage and he will have permission to do whatever he wants here – change the furniture, whatever. This is his house. He is my brother.

"As gay people we tend to distance ourselves from our families. It's sad and we've been pushed to do that, because who wants to be around a hostile society? But we need to make a little effort to work with our families, to show and teach our families to accept us and to see us as valuable people. I had to teach my own family to accept me so I know that it's hard. It wasn't easy for me to accept myself – why should it be easy for them? Still, I believe we have that responsibility."

ROBERTO GARCIA

40, director of AIDS service organization

"I was born in Brownsville, Texas. My dad worked as a cotton compressor on a cotton gin and my mom was a homemaker. Most of my family is still in Texas. I have two sisters here in California who accept me. It took work, but they're open to me. The rest of my family is pretty much out of the picture. It's pretty painful for me so I keep them at a distance.

"When someone accepts you for who you are, it's wonderful – like my straight friend who hugs me and cares for me. I asked him the other day, 'Why are you so cool?' And he said, 'Well, I have different values for a Latino person.' The Latino culture is very closed to gay people; it's taboo. But he learned differently from his family. Latino culture has terrible values

Left to right: Adriana Lopez, Carlos Lopez and Tony Lopez, brothers and sister-in-law.
Above: Robert watches his sister, Carmen, prepare quesadillas.

at times. They can restrict you from being the human being you want to be.

"I've created my own values of what being a man means. When I look at my upbringing, and how my family treated me, I can see why I had to gather my own value system. I knew I could, partly because I'm in recovery, and I had to do it.

"I have a son and a daughter. I just became a grandfather last week. I don't have any contact with my daughter – her mother had a very hard time when I came out – but I am in touch with my son. I don't know if he knows about my life, but I know there are rumors about me in Brownsville, where he lives, so I assume he knows.

"My family now is my two sisters, who are very close to me. Carmen is here today, and we are trying to get my other sister from Los Angeles to move up here. But my family is also Victor's family. They treat me very well. I'm very close to his mother. I spent my vacation with her. I have my own room there, and I've asked her to come live with us.

"I want to spend the rest of my life with Victor, but I need to allow both of us to grow up. We are very solid, though, and we have closed the 'back-door' option of leaving the relationship. We don't talk about that as an option anymore."

OLIVIA GOMEZ

28, homemaker & Jorge Gomez, 28, restaurant manager

"We are from Mexico City. We've been married almost five years. We have known Roberto and Victor for almost two years. We saw an ad asking for volunteers for Shanti Project [a local AIDS service organization], so we went down and met Roberto and Victor at the training. We liked the way they treated people.

"We don't like when some people say the AIDS is only gay people, or the AIDS is only this and this. The AIDS is a sickness and you have to be there to help a little, to make more people understand what all this is about. We wanted to help.

"We are not afraid of gay people – why? They are not afraid of us. We are Mormons, and you know how a lot of people in the church are; but no, we do not hate gay people. My church tells me if you have someone outside who wants to be your friend, it doesn't matter who it is, or how other people call him. If he wants to be your friend, you should be his friend. We have been having a lot of problems with people telling us we are different from our Latino culture, too. And this is true. I know from my own people, they hate gay people and say they want to kill them.

"But our fathers gave us a different education. Since I was around ten, my mother went to a beauty shop where there were only gay people. My mom said she went there because they are the best, so I started knowing them. I had a lot on my mind because my friends were telling me not to

Victor with his friends Olivia and Jorge Gomez.

Husband and wife, Carmen and Marco share a family meal with Victor.

go, but I did it anyway. And I washed dishes, I cooked and look! I am not gay. My mom told me the gays are people like you and me — they are free to be as they like. I think that sometimes being gay is not a choice.

"To us, to be part of this family is a great honor. We have our own families, but we've known them since we were born. Love is the word that can tell you everything."

CARMEN LOPEZ

37, cook

"At first, I was upset when I found out Roberto was gay. I remember not talking to him for a couple of months. He would come and visit me

and I wouldn't open the door. But my husband talked to me about it a lot and so I called Roberto one day and we started seeing each other again. We're the closest ones, always, but after that we got closer. I get along well with Victor and I don't get embarrassed anymore. And my sons still say Roberto's their uncle. There are others in my family who don't talk to him since they found out — my four brothers and my mother. She still has that anger on her.

"In my family, there's a lot of anger. Once they get mad, they won't talk to you. Right now, I don't want to go to Texas, because I know my brothers will say something about Roberto and I don't want to argue with them about it. Roberto is my oldest brother and I always respected him. He was always on my side whenever I needed him. He will listen to me when I have problems and I know my other brothers won't do that. It's a macho thing.

"If I could talk to my brothers, I would say: forget about the past. We only live once. Sooner or later, one of us will not be here. You can't tell someone to be someone they can't be."

Roberto and his nephew Carlos kill time while waiting for dinner.

HOW TO MAKE A FAMILY

LETI GOMEZ AND SABRINA SOJOURNER'S FAMILY
Washington, D.C.

Saturday night in the northeast section of the District – it's mid September and still warm. We arrive just as Leti Gomez, the guest of honor, arrives looking freshly showered and harried. Sabrina Sojourner is throwing a birthday party for Leti, her partner of three years. The party is supposed to start at seven, so by six, Sabrina and Leti, and Leti's mom Angelina and her partner Robert have come to Liane and Linda's house to start setting up. Liane and Linda have just finished cleaning. They go upstairs to shower. Leti and Robert begin getting the drinks on ice. Someone turns on music. Sabrina stirs a hot pot of queso. Angelina samples and pronounces approval.

By the time Geoff and I leave at midnight, the party is still going strong. It has been a success – people laughing, dancing and dishing, political and personal. José has come and performed a torch song, in Spanish and in drag, to a rapt Leti and her mother. Everything seems fluid and easy, not at all intentional or by design, but in fact, the party, and the family Leti and Sabrina have brought together, are all of those things. They chose to commit to each other, for "however long forever is," as Leti said. And they continue to choose family to spend time with, and make holidays with, deliberately.

While they are doing so, they have fun. This is a family that dances together and eats together, where people go out of their way to be respectful and kind, not only with their in-laws but also with each other. They check in with each other on a regular basis; they have dinners and long talks; they cry and support each other; and they celebrate together, as they do on this night of Leti's 40th birthday, long into the night and well into memory, because this is how families are made, with love and will.

LETI GOMEZ

40, director of a national gay & lesbian organization and civil servant

"I work two jobs: I'm the executive director of LLEGO, which is the national Latino/a lesbian and gay organization, and I work part-time for the federal government. Being the activists we are, Sabrina and I met at the first 'Creating Change' conference that the NGLTF [National Gay and Lesbian Task Force] had here in D.C., but I don't really remember meeting her. My first clear recollection of Sabrina is later, at another conference. She was reading erotic poetry and she had everyone's attention. I walked in late and sat down and she read a poem about women in flannel shirts. I was wearing a flannel shirt, and it caught my attention.

"When she moved to Washington, we got to be friends. That's what was different for me; I had ventured into relationships without establishing a friendship with lovers before, so when the lust was gone, I thought, 'Well, what do I have?' The chemistry was all there with Sabrina but we were friends initially, and that made it a lot more interesting.

"I had confirmation one evening. It was a hot September night here in D.C. and we were at her house. She had the fan on and the door open and

1) Rena Regna
2) JoAnna Regna
3) Keith Boylin,
4) Robert Segovia
5) Elena Calle
6) Ruth Miller,
7) Angelina Gomez
8) Sonia Henry
9) Leti Gomez,
10) Patricia Montes
11) Robert Foster
12) Sabrina Sojourner
13) Alexander Robinson
14) Linda
15) Liane
16) Al Lawrence
17) Antonio
18) Phyllis Turner
19) Barbara Garcia

we were lying down, kissing. All of a sudden, I heard the fan fall over and I looked up and saw a man in the doorway. Now, I didn't have my glasses on and I'm blind as a bat without my glasses, but I jumped up and just went after him without thinking, and chased him away. And later, I realized, if I did all that without my glasses, there must really be something there.

"I have a need to be connected to people and not feel isolated. Even within the relationship, it's just the two of us and I feel the need to be connected to something larger. I've thought about moving back to Texas just so I could be closer to my blood family.

"I'm very close to my biological family. I'm now the oldest, and the only girl. I have three living brothers. After I had just started being with Sabrina, I went home for a two week visit and I took a photograph of her home with me so my

mother and brothers could see her, because I wanted to bring her home for Christmas. I had never brought a black woman home and I wanted to make sure there weren't going to be any problems. But my mom said 'Oh, she looks beautiful! We'd be glad to have her.' And my brothers were also welcoming.

"I had not seriously ever considered having a commitment ceremony, but after talking about it with Sabrina, it became very clear to me that I wanted one. The ceremony was done by an African-American professor of theology at Howard who speaks Spanish and who is an expert in African-American traditions. We wrote the ceremony. It included African and Indian and Chicano traditions. We walked in to African drumming and walked out to mariachi music. Both our families participated. At the end, everyone stood up and came all around us, raised their hands, and committed to us and the relationship.

"So far, it's been great. Every couple has their moments, but for the very first time, in all of my relationships, I know, 'Well, if it gets tough, we're going to have to deal with it.' Leaving may be the option of last resort, but it's not the first option anymore.

"I came from a single-parent family that was very loving, and I find that family under attack. And now, Sabrina and I are creating this other family that is also under attack. I think of all the people who are in our family, both blood and chosen, and they are all productive, wonderful people. To think that there is a movement underfoot in this country to undermine that family, working to destroy it and exclude us, is very painful.

"And it makes me very angry. Our gay and

lesbian community hasn't really dealt with this attack. Our families are just as valuable and just as loving as any other. All the basic human needs and love are all there, they are just framed differently."

SABRINA SOJOURNER
42, writer and diversity consultant

"I had the maddest crush on this woman for years, but could never catch her attention. She was in one of my workshops, and we ran into each other later and talked, but it was just like – nothing there. Leti was in a relationship at that time. The nice thing about that for me now is that I know other women may raise an eyebrow now and again, but they won't be able to get her attention.

"It wasn't until I moved here to Washington that we really got to know each other. I was floored when, some months later, Leti told me she was attracted to me. I'd given up on getting even a serious look in the eye from this one. But we had already gotten into this very comfortable routine of seeing each other once a week and talking on the telephone at least twice a week, whether we were in town or not. And so we felt like family long before we slept together.

"On Labor Day Weekend of '91, we finally got our act together and proposed to each other. After we started being sexual, and having a wonderful time, she went away for about two weeks. We talked on the phone every day when she was gone. The night she came back, she came over to my apartment, and I had every candle I owned lit for her. I had a bottle of champagne and it was chilled and waiting, and I don't think we even had dinner.

"While she was gone it became clear that this was

something that was going to last. We had talked about commitment before, and I had told her that I was tired of, 'Oh, we'll be together as long as everything is okay.' That was a big yawn for me. I wanted someone who was willing to work through the hard stuff. So that night, we decided that we wanted to have a ceremony to have others acknowledge our commitment to each other. It took us a long time to decide when to have it, but I realized that a lot of people all over the country really loved us, and suddenly it hit me that we should do it Saturday night before the March [The April, 1993 March on Washington for Lesbian, Gay, and Bi Equal Rights and Liberation]. And that's what we did. A little over 220 people came.

"We got calls from her brother who was in France, and cards from three of my four sisters that day. We had a lot of fun. I wore a black lace dress: long, handkerchief hemline, with lace and chiffon, and satin bows and sequins. Leti had a suit made, ivory gabardine wool, with a layered shawl collar, that she wore with a turquoise shell. Our attendants walked in first. After them came Robert and Leti's mother, and then Leti walked in with her brother, and then my two friends walked in and I walked in with my 22-year-old son.

"I believe that a wedding ceremony is an opportunity to say to the spirits, to the ancestors, and to all the people you care about, that this is the person I care about and I am making a commitment to for the rest of my life, and who I love with all of my heart. There may be times when I lose sight of that, and I want their remembrance to get me through those hard times.

"For me, family is an emotional and spiritual commitment to be there for someone. It means if this person needs something, and I can do some-

Above left: Sabrina with friends Alexander and Robert.
Above right: Leti and her mother Angelina.

thing about it, be it just listening or providing them with the resources by which to bring something about, I will do that.

"There are a lot of ways in which that plays out. Sometimes, it really is just about listening. Other times, it's about saying, 'I'm sorry that happened to you,' or saying, 'You know, that person is really a shit for doing that to you – do you want me to go beat them up?' Even if you don't intend to do that, it often feels good just to hear somebody else be outraged. But family is also a commitment to challenge and to prod, where with an acquaintance, you may not want to jeopardize the relationship. There's nobody I consider family that I also feel like I couldn't say, 'What the hell is going on?' That's important, and I expect it back from them. And I get it.

"For five years, I was really estranged from the family I was raised in. Just this year, my mother and I have started speaking again on a regular basis. Now, she's being very accepting of Leti. My mother and my mother's sister Thelma have made a point of inviting Leti and me to the family reunion. It's in Huntsville, Texas, and we are definitely going.

"But for some number of years, she just couldn't deal with me. The excuse was about me being a lesbian, but the real reason was that my mother couldn't deal with her own shit about my being abused. It was easier for her to blame her feelings on me being a lesbian; she wanted to link the abuse and my lesbianism together. Now, I don't have the expectation of her being a mother the way I need a mother. I have other women in my life that I get that from.

"We don't just see the people in our family at meetings or whatever. We make a point to check with them, for every family event, like birthdays and holidays, to make sure that if they're in town, we'll do something together. We also try to check in at least every few weeks. It's very intentional.

"I know that this is in direct reaction to growing up in such a dysfunctional family. I don't believe that family, inherently, is evil, just as I don't believe that nothing good came out of my dysfunctional family. There's something very powerful about being bonded to other people. I've gotten to a point in my own life where I can take care of myself much more than I used to be able to, but I know I've really arrived because I finally have people I'm not afraid to ask for help from.

"When we talk about families, we must focus the discussion on the values of that family, not who is in it. Respect for others; appreciation of differ-

ences; value of life; a sense of history and a sense of culture; self-respect and respect for the community with an understanding that you give back to the community – those are the values that we are imparting. As long as we're having a figurehead discussion (who's in the family or not), then the discussion will be about keeping some people in and some people out. If we were to have a value-centered discussion about family, I think we would have much more agreement than disagreement."

ANGELINA GOMEZ
68, homemaker

"I'm Leti's mom and she's my only daughter. I was praying for a daughter. She was a beautiful baby and she's a beautiful human being. Like any mother, at the beginning it was hard when I found out she was a lesbian. But I love her and I accept her. There is no question in my mind. A mother's love is unconditional. She's my baby, even though she's 40 years old today. And Sabrina's a very nice woman. They seem to get along and my daughter's happy. What can I say? I'm satisfied with my daughter. She has made a good life for herself.

"People from my culture, if they did have children like mine, they probably would hide it. Nobody has ever asked me about Leti or Sabrina. They don't ask, so I don't say, but if they did ask, I would say."

ALEXANDER ROBINSON
37, organizer and activist

"Having women in my life is important to me, and being able to have women who understand and accept my partner and want us to be there together is important. The reason the public believes that there aren't long-term gay relation-

Angelina moved to tears of joy.

ships is because we're here, in someone's home, enjoying our family time together.

"I didn't have a great relationship with my biological family, so I have gone about my life creating family for myself. I think that people do that all the time. I grew up in an African-American community where I had brothers and sisters, aunts and uncles that were not biological, and I still have those kinds of relationships with those people. I don't think that gay and lesbian folks are that different about those kinds of things.

"Gay and lesbian people form all kinds of families. For example, with transvestites, these are people who know what you look like without the wig and they will help you and back you up. We've had to form families to protect ourselves."

ROBERT FOSTER
36, attorney

"A lot of gay people make their way in the world by leaving family behind, but Sabrina and Leti are not that way. I think that it's not necessary for gay people to imitate what straight people have. Alexander and I don't refer to our intimate friends as our family, because for me, that would be like trying to be like a straight person and it wouldn't feel honest. But that's not what it is for Sabrina and Leti. They can talk about their marriage, which was a beautiful and moving event, and for them, it's like a glorious celebration.

"A lot of times, I come to these family events, like a holiday or birthday, or wedding or something, and I'm the only white man there, and that's an interesting and valuable experience for me. Men aren't the focus at these gatherings and neither are white people in the majority. But I've never felt

picked on or put in a corner with Sabrina and Leti, and I am capable of feeling that way. I think that's remarkable. Sabrina and Leti are both very talented, smart people, so it's flattering to be included. At their wedding, I had the sense that they would stay together for a long, long time, because it was clear that one plus one was more than two with them."

"ANTONIO [1]"
43, mortgage supervisor

"I come from a very large family of twelve kids and I am the youngest. As a Latino, coming from where I did in the Southwest, there were a lot of things that happened. My mom died when I was an infant and my father had to deal with all of us kids. And there was a lot of poverty and a lot of racism and discrimination that created a lot of problems for us. In our family, we all had to depend on each other and be supportive of each other. And I carry that to my gay friends, especially now, in the last ten years.

"I have a personal relationship with God. He knows who I am and what I've done. I have basic Christian values that have been with me all my life, and God recognizes them. The Pope and the Vatican are wrong and hypocritical. They have used us as scapegoats to redirect attention from their own real problems. God loves gay people. We do a lot of good for this whole world. I know it because I'm living it."

"LUIS [1]"
44, computer instructor

"I don't think about the length of time 'Antonio' and I have been together [21 years]; it's just a

natural thing. Compromise is the key. There are enough people who want to be together and want to be in love, but because we all want to be individuals and we don't want to compromise, we don't make it even when we do care about each other. I hope Leti and Sabrina have a lasting relationship, but one that's happy. It's no good having a lasting relationship if it's not happy.

"What keeps heterosexual couples together is often this institution of marriage and children, which gives them a social pressure to be together. When you find gay people who have been together for a long period, it's even more amazing, because they don't have that social pressure to pull them together. They have everything fighting to pull them apart. But ultimately, it's the same — two people working to stay together and make a better life for themselves.

"It actually wasn't until the Republicans made such a big deal about family values that I stopped and realized we were part of the people they were talking about. My life is very normal and natural; when you're in a family, you don't have to stop and think about it — it's just there. 'Antonio' and I were a family before we even thought about it, and being part of Leti and Sabrina's family is natural too. A lot of gay people have family without even knowing it."

LIANE
33, video producer

"Before I was ten, we lived in a largely Jewish neighborhood. Our big distinction was that we were gentiles, not that we were black. My father has been very accepting and calls Linda his second daughter, and my mother is coming around to

---

[1] *"Antonio" and "Luis" are pseudonyms.*

thinking of us as a family. They've asked if we were getting married!

"At my brother's wedding, I was a bridesmaid, and I kept wondering what is Linda's position and what is her role. I felt self-conscious about it. She did kind of stick out, because it was primarily black people there. I've never really had this conversation with my brother, so it was sort of awkward and inhibiting and hard. I didn't feel like we could just be us in this setting.

"I'd like to be able to have Linda's picture on my desk at work and not have anybody think twice about it. I have a picture of one of our kitties, but it's not the same. I'd like to be able to have conversations with people about what I did and who I was with and it would be understood who she was to me. I wouldn't have to explain, or feel like I was hiding. I'd like to not feel any hesitation,

to share as freely as any straight person."

LINDA

42, video producer, owner of a production company

"Family and responsibility to family has always been part of my cultural background as a Chicana. Living away from my family, I've tried to recreate family here. I have to, to feel comfortable. I need to have friends who feel like brothers and sisters. Liane is my partner, and although we're not ready for a commitment ceremony, we're very committed.

"I feel very close to Leti because of our shared background as Mexican-Americans, so when she said she was going to have a birthday party at her new house, a few days after she moved, I said, 'No, you're not. You'll have it here.' To me, that's what family does. Sometimes you push yourself. This house was a disaster, but we got it ready.

"It's been difficult with my blood family. I'd been disowned by my family over other things in the past, so over twenty years ago, when I had my first woman lover, I decided I wouldn't tell them. It's an awful bind for me. On some level my mother and dad know, and they know and like Liane, so I think on some level they accept it. They understand, emotionally, but I think if I said the word, they wouldn't be able to handle it. I wish I was at the point where I didn't care, but it's not worth risking it.

"If they still loved me after I told them, it would be such a tremendous relief; I could be me. I wouldn't be so afraid. If they still loved me, it would mean I was loveable, and acceptable, and I could love myself. Mostly, it would mean I could feel safe. We don't feel safe enough even to hold hands in most public places. I don't feel safe in this world."

YOLANDA SANTIAGO

45, computer systems analyst

"Everybody has family. We don't come in a vacuum and we don't leave in a vacuum. I am Puerto Ricana, which is very important to me. The tradition of family is very strong for me. It's the place you can go to rescue yourself when everything is terrible. People will lick your wounds and comfort you and embrace you. If you don't have family, you have nothing.

"Every human being has the right to have love. For gay and lesbian people, we have been told we are not entitled to have those rights. Let me give you an example. In English, you have the word 'lovers.' I hate that word, because lovers is somebody who you share sex with, but it's not someone you share life with. 'Compañeras' in Spanish is a better word. It's somebody you are going to share with, a friend, a lover, a spouse. It's like a spouse, but more deep.

"Leti is the godmother of my child. Sabrina is going to present her to the community soon. It's very important that he have all the goodwill of family, all the nurture, so he can go to the outside and say, 'Yes, I have this. I have love from all these people.' That's what we all need. The non-religious right says they have family values, but family values are love, and that's what we have. True, this family is a little untraditional, but I was raised by a single mother, and everybody in my neighborhood was raised by a single parent, and everybody was okay because they all got love from the extended family. And my son will have the same."

Angelina dances with her daughter on her 40th birthday.

Salsa dancing into the night.

HOW LONG DOES LOVE LAST?

SHARON KOWALSKI, KAREN THOMPSON AND PATTY BRESSER
Clearwater, Minnesota

They had had a good day with the kids, as always. Sharon Kowalski adored her niece and nephew, and Karen Thompson was not worried when Sharon left to drive the kids home. It had been a family day, and Karen was content. They'd been together four years, had struggled to a painful, private recognition of their sexual orientation, and found in each other a love they knew would last. In a parking lot one night, they exchanged rings, said vows — it was as close to God as their church would let them get. Still, they believed in the future.

But after Sharon's car was hit by a drunk driver that night, she was so injured she was unable to make herself understood in conventional ways. And because their marriage was not legally recognized, it took Karen eight years to bring Sharon home. Eight years and lawsuits all the way to the Minnesota Supreme Court before she was allowed to take care of Sharon in the dedicated and determined way her love demanded that she do. Eight years of excruciating tests of her love, of having to come out publicly despite her Midwest reserve and political reticence, so she could gather the support and financial backing to fight those who had kept her from even seeing her partner for four of those eight years.

Sharon and Karen had known Patty Bresser

before she moved away, a year before the accident, and they had kept in touch. When Karen saw Patty after a speech seven years later, the two women realized they had a lot to talk about, and began a correspondence. Without wanting to,

A plaque in the bathroom.

they had fallen in love. Karen cautioned Patty that she would never leave Sharon, but Patty already understood that. Two years later, when Patty moved back to Minnesota to live with Karen and Sharon, it was clear she was coming not only to be with Karen, but also to care for Sharon. Today, the three of them live quietly along the banks of the Mississippi River, where Sharon had once loved to fish, in a new home built with the facilities Sharon needs. Sharon still wears Karen's ring. Patty and Karen are devoted to her, and to each other. How long does love last? At least for this lifetime, and into the next.

KAREN THOMPSON
47, professor

"When Patty and I renewed our friendship, we had no clue that there would be anything more than that. She knew that I loved Sharon and would never walk away from her. I'm a person who comes with so much baggage I find it difficult to believe that anyone could love me for who I am today, and also know that I'll never leave Sharon. When I made a commitment to Sharon, I meant for it to be for a lifetime. And I probably love her more today than I loved her then. With every breath I take, I love this woman. And yet, I found we're capable of more love, and different kinds of love, than I ever knew.

"I've had to struggle with everything I believe in, but it's been so long now, it's not a conflict anymore. Neither love takes away from the other love. Sharon, Patty and I constitute a family. We've found this to be very workable. Without Patty, there's no way I could have Sharon home. I didn't look for Patty in order to bring Sharon home — it just happened — but it turned out to be very healthy for all of us. Without Sharon here, it really wasn't home to me.

"After years of fighting for Sharon in every way I knew how, in December of 1991, the Appellate

with adequate care. I know I simply must let go of that pain, and the rage I feel that the court system let that happen. It's been ten years since the accident, and we're probably not going to make a lot of progress. I haven't given up, though. In my heart, I hurt every time I look at her, how these people condemned her to this quality of life. There were twenty appeals to the state court, and twenty times they upheld the rights of the guardian to do this to her.

"I've watched Sharon and tried to see if

anything's hurting her about our family today, and I don't see it. She laughs with Patty, and they are very good for each other. They have the same sense of humor. They're developing their own relationship, separate from me. Day in and day out, Patty can accept the depth of my relationship with Sharon and it's not threatening to her. It still amazes me. And what she gives Sharon is amazing. We've been very open with our relationship; we've been all over the country together. I'm through with hiding.

Court for the State of Minnesota finally ruled Sharon and I were a family of affinity that should be accorded respect. That finding sets a precedent, even though it's in Minnesota, because there is no legal language like that anywhere else. But when the case was sent back to the district court, with instructions to grant me complete guardianship, Judge Campbell would never sign the order. The chief judge of the district finally signed it. Judge Campbell obviously had some personal investment in the case, but we never knew what it was, and shortly thereafter, he resigned as a judge. It took until August of 1992 for me to get the actual papers so I could do something about bringing Sharon home. Obviously, I was hoping the case would break years before it did. I never dreamed it would take clear until 1992 to get those papers.

"I had the house built so Sharon could be as independent as possible. The hardest thing for me has been that the case didn't break open in time to get Sharon the help she needed. There was a window of time for her to regain some skills, and that window was lost. Now we'll never know what Sharon could have done if she had been provided

Sharon communicates with Karen using her computer.

"Sharon lost so much, years of her life imprisoned. She's paid dearly for people's fear and ignorance. She's been blossoming here. Her doctor said she was thriving, and I realized that when Sharon thrives, I thrive. It makes me feel so good that she can live and form relationships with other people. That's what I fought for.

"Even before the accident, Sharon taught me how to live, and how to love. She's teaching me now to make this moment as high a quality of moment as we have. We live our life right now, being as happy as can be, right now. Because we don't know if there's a tomorrow.

"People may judge us, but I don't live in the right/wrong anymore. We can all be different, and all be okay.

"I don't dwell too much on the future. I think the idea that change takes time somehow immobilizes us. Obviously, I'd like to see a time in the future when we're more pluralistic in our way of viewing each other, when we can get away from this one up/one down position.

"I've learned I must take care of myself too, in order to have something to give Sharon. I've given to myself that it's okay to love Patty and to receive what I can from her. And I love her very much, very differently from Sharon. But Patty's helped me find the ability to laugh and play, to find time for us to do things together. It's a juggling act sometimes, to know that it's okay for Sharon to go into respite care so Patty and I can have a weekend together. If I'm not going to burn out, if I'm going to be in this for the long haul, it's got to be okay. Patty helps me refuel and go on. I don't know what I'd do without her. I'm a fortunate person to have two very special people who love me very much.

"Learning to reach out and ask for help, and learning that I couldn't do this all by myself, was very humbling for me. People have been wonderful to us. In the beginning people sent one and two dollar bills. I've received love and support from all over the country.

"I want Patty to be happy too, to fly. She's a person who gives and gives. I wear two rings now. The ring Sharon gave me I will always wear. But I wear Patty's ring too, and both rings are very deep commitments I have made."

Patty plays the electric piano.

Patty and Karen shoot some hoops while Sharon looks on.

PATTY BRESSER

39, nurse and teacher

"I knew both Karen and Sharon fifteen years ago when I worked out here, but I went back to Connecticut in 1981. I called Karen as soon as I heard that Sharon had an accident. We were all pretty closeted at the time, but we all knew she and Sharon were together. After that, we lost track of each other, although I always sent a Christmas card. Then in 1990, I heard Karen was coming to Connecticut to speak, so I called her. Things progressed such that by 1992 I moved out here to be with her. We're in a committed relationship now – we've exchanged rings. I knew that Karen had a prior commitment to Sharon, and so, in a way, I committed to both of them.

"Karen and Sharon had been separated for almost four years, after Sharon's father became her guardian and got a court order to keep Karen from seeing her.

"My family thinks I'm crazy. It's difficult to explain. We're different, but this family unit works for us. Sharon and I are friends, and we were before the accident. Sharon is so unique, and she's one of the nicest people I ever met. What you see with her is what you get. She lives now only in the moment. But if you're a friend of Sharon's, you're a friend for life. I always thought the world of her, and I still do. Karen has asked Sharon multiple times, in many different ways, if it is okay with her that I live here, and Sharon has always said yes.

"And I'm happy here. I love Karen, and I want to be with her. I can't really describe it. We just fell in love and we didn't know what hit either one of us. We struggled with it for almost two years because we didn't know what we were doing. But we finally decided the least we could do was give it a shot.

"We have to protect ourselves legally. We have durable powers of attorney for each other but I worry about what would happen to Sharon if something happens to Karen. Karen tells me she would become a ward of the state. I can't be legally named successor guardian, but I would want that responsibility because I consider Sharon family. I don't know that there is anyone else who would, or could, take care of her. I would defer to anyone she wanted, if there was anyone else she wanted.

"Here, there's a lot of love, a lot of trust, honesty, and emotional support. It's safe here. We don't have to hide anything. We give and take a lot from one another. This family, for us, is much more functional than the ones we came from. Maybe we learned some lessons along the way, and certainly because of what Karen and Sharon have gone through, we learned some things.

"Sharon amazes me on a daily basis. She has such courage. I look at what she has gone through – the sheer isolation, institutional abandonment, surgery, lack of physical care – and she still kept her wits about her. She has not just survived. She has strength. She appreciates life, even after everything. She can't get away from what's happened. She can't remember things that happened five minutes ago, and still can't use the left side of her body. But she's very much a part of what's happening around her. It's the biggest victory."

Sharon gets a tube feeding before the 1994 Minnesota Gay Pride Parade.

Karen, Sharon and Patty march through Minneapolis with the Central Minnesota Lesbian contingent.

MEETING THE QUEEN

BILL SPENCER AND STEVEN STEINBOCK'S FAMILY
Portland, Oregon

As it turns out, Geoff and I have come to have lunch with the royalty of the Rose Court of the Inland Empire, only we don't know that yet. I have a vague notion these men might do drag, maybe on weekends. I am not prepared to meet Champagne, the Empress XXV, nor Empress XXXII, called Velvet, and his Emperor, Mr. Bill, and I don't realize that one of our hosts is Empress XXXV.

For many years, drag queens were worse than an embarrassment to me – I felt they were pretending to be women in a way I found demeaning. Each year at the pride parades I watched the bitchy, high-heeled stereotype on display and I saw them on television that night and in the morning paper, and each year I wished they would go away.

Of course, I didn't actually know any drag queens then, and I probably wouldn't have known any at all, except for AIDS. As it turned out, I found myself taking ballroom dance lessons with a remarkable and respectful man who had been caring for his sick partner for several years – it was my job to get him out of the house at least once a week. One night, as we were learning to grapevine a fox trot, he explained he had shaved his beard that weekend to do drag. At my stunned look, he went on to talk about masks and freedom, the need to look from another perspective and the honor of representing his feminine side. I was concentrating

on my footwork when he whispered, "It's still me."

I don't know that I yet understand the attraction of doing drag, nor its mystery. But I understand that the elaborate network of the Imperial Court has raised much money for AIDS and other gay organizations. And I understand drag is not really about women at all, but about men who are willing

to see all of themselves. These are dedicated families of strong men who spend their time caring for each other and passing along their craft, brother to brother. And perhaps all I really need to understand is that love dresses in whatever clothes are required.

BILL SPENCER

32, retail sales, Empress XXXV

"The Court is a charitable and social fund raising organization that's been in existence here in the Portland area for over thirty years. The Court system started in San Francisco and since then, it's branched out all over the United States and Canada. Mainly, it's just groups of people who get together. Not everybody's doing drag. People do different kinds of looks, like leather people or gay women doing a more masculine look, formal or motorcycle or leather, and of course, all different kinds of drag queens: glamorous, pretty drag queens; fun, comedy drag queens; drag queens who do celebrities; and drag queens who look like themselves.

"So this big diverse group of people gets together and holds coronations in each of the cities, to have fun and to raise money. There are various functions and events, parties and picnics, barbeques and different types of fund raising shows and activities. In most of the cities, it started out with just the Empress. But then, in some cities, the job got to be too big for one person, so they decided to have an Emperor title. It was a way to include men who didn't do drag, and also women. I was Empress 35, the Flawless White Diamond of the

Left to right in Bill and Steven's kitchen, Jeff Taylor, W.R. Dumbrowski, Duane "Champagne" Brooks, Paul Milton, Leonard Westberg, Steven Steinbock, and Bill Spenc

Rose Court. My drag name is Michelle Craig.

"The Court is exactly like the Masons, or the Elks Club, but it's for gay people. You know how they dress up and run for Queen of the Masons, like that? Well, it's very similar. They have big parties, and people have a lot of fun, and they raise a lot of money for charity.

"I've been dressing up since I was a little boy, wearing costumes and funny hats. And I always knew I was gay. In high school, I was very involved in the theater. A lot of people in the Court or who do drag, started out in the theater. Right now, dressing up is a hobby of mine, but it's a small part of my whole life. Steve is not married to Michelle Craig. He's married to Bill.

"Steve was my first serious relationship, and I've been involved with him for all of my adult life, since I was twenty. We've been together for

Steven helps Michelle with her dress.
Above and left: Bill and Jeff become Michelle and Jenny Craig.

Michelle sprays the hair of her 'daughter

twelve years now, and we definitely see ourselves as married — I call him my husband and we always joke that we should have had a ceremony so we could have gotten the gifts.

"It's not true that gay relationships don't last. The gentleman who was Emperor when I was Empress has been with his lover almost 30 years. And I know a lot more messed-up heterosexual couples and marriages than I do gay people. One of the problems is that the right-wingers are so hung up on the sex part. They seem to think everything revolves around sex. But sex is a small part of our relationship. There's the everyday routine, and our small problems, just like everybody else. The first five years are the hardest, but if you just let your relationship develop, and it's the right person, after awhile, you'll know. Honesty has worked for us, and deciding things together, planning. And respect. That sense of having someone there for me all the time has been really important for me."

STEVEN STEINBOCK

37, retail manager

"Being married is very comfortable, knowing that when I come home, there'll be someone I can talk to, somebody I can spend my time with. Our family is Bill and myself, Jasper and Panda, our Boston terriers, and our bird, Petey. We own our home. We bought it together, and we share our expenses.

"I do most of the cooking, and the yard. But we each do what we're good at. I love being home. I don't see any point in having a wedding ceremony because we've been together for so long.

"Of course we fight. Everybody fights. But anymore, it's over something trivial, and we

Left to right at the ball: Michelle Craig, Steven Steinbock, Champagne, Paul Milton, and Jenny Craig.

Michelle lip synchs. The microphone is just for show.

usually end up laughing about it later. Fifteen or twenty minutes later, we're on to something else. We've never had that serious of a problem. And I count on us always being together.

"The people coming over today are also in our family. It seems like we've known them forever. We can tell them anything. We're with them almost every weekend, and on holidays. I'm close to my biological family, too, and for the last ten years, we've had both my family and Bill's family over for Thanksgiving.

"I was very proud of Bill when he was Empress, and the drag he does. I've had a wonderful time living with him, and loving him. It's made me grow up, being together and accepting responsibility."

LEONARD WESTBURG

38, display coordinator, Empress XXXII

"I was the Sweetheart of Portland, and Mr. Bill was my Emperor. I've known Bill and Steve for about 13 years. For a while, I lived in the same building with them and I was always over for dinner. Now I'm with Paul and we're both part of their family and we love them.

"Family is about respect. I was in a bad relationship for about seven years, but never once did this family say to me that I should leave. They respected me enough to let me make my own decisions."

CHAMPAGNE

35, hairdresser, Empress XXV

"I was Portland Empress XXV, the Celebration of the Rose. Mr. Bill and I have been together for fourteen years and we've known Bill and Steven for twelve.

"One time, I was attending a drag function in Colorado Springs, Colorado, and there was a bunch of protesters outside. They came up and told me I was going to burn in hell. I asked them how they knew I wasn't here just to test them, to see how willing they were to love and to see how non-judgmental they were. God made me, and obviously put me here for a reason. They just stood there and looked at me. They had no response.

"They can say, 'Bad, bad,' but I don't think they realize what they're doing. I remember different parts of the Bible than they do, obviously. They're trying to destroy people, and you can't really talk to them about it. I think they're using us as a meal ticket. But why fight us? We're not trying to take over. It's not like we want special rights. We just want the same rights. I've never seen this 'gay agenda' thing. Have you?

"What I do in my bedroom doesn't make them better people. If they don't have anything going for them, they can say, 'Well, at least I'm straight.' But I try to make the world a better place. And I look around and wonder what they're doing."

THE ART IN SURVIVAL

LEOTA LONE DOG'S FAMILY
Brooklyn, New York

Jean and I sit in the car on a Brooklyn street and wait for Leota Lone Dog. She is one of these incredibly busy people who gets up before dawn and drags herself home late at night. We are lucky to have reserved a little spot in her schedule.

Up to the gate walks a woman in blue jeans, a white shirt, and a paisley vest. She looks preoccupied but not rushed. Jean says, "That's her." We get out of the car. She has just come from the subway. I know how hard it is to make appointments on time when you rely on the trains. She is a beautiful woman with a warm air of confidence about her, and she ushers us upstairs into her home.

At the time of this interview Leota lived with her invalid mother and her 15-year-old niece. Her mother has since died, but today she lies on a bed in the kitchen-dining room. The cluttered entry room is where we conduct our interview; French doors separate it from a closet-sized studio where, Leota, an art history graduate student, does her painting. During the interview the niece rushes in from school and we grab a quick photo before she rushes back out again.

As Jean conducts her interview, there is no place for me to go; and I find few things to photograph. It occurs to me that my function here is not to record with the camera, but to listen to the words. For this is the oral history of a twentieth century

Native American lesbian. It is a tale told by a sage and a survivor. It is a story of possibility.

LEOTA LONE DOG
47, artist /art history student

"I identify as Two-Spirited; my tribal affiliation is Lakota, Mohawk and Delaware, but I'm enrolled as Lakota, Oglala, on the Rosebud Reservation. I have been told I would be considered middle class because I have an education, even though we lived in a welfare hotel, and I had no clothes, and food was scarce.

"I was born in Manhattan, and shortly after, my parents left and went to California. We travelled back and forth between the West Coast and here because my father was always trying to find work. He was drinking a lot. Eventually, we got back here, and he went back to the reservation.

"My mother and my sister and I stayed with my uncle for a while, then we moved to a hotel on 49th Street. When we lived with my uncle, we were not only the only Indians, we were the only dark-skinned people there. I was constantly called names – dirty Indian, nigger, or spic – whatever was negative, they called me.

"My grandmother said we should just go and tell them they were dirty white trash, but that had no power in it for me. The images I got from home

about who we were as Native Americans didn't hold up against the onslaught of what society said we were. What held power were those names, because I internalized and accepted those images of myself.

"Plus, my mother was a seer. That disrupted our entire home life. Whenever we would be home, there would be people waiting for readings. There was no place for us to do our homework, or live, or be. So we were out on the street a lot. My mother went in and out of mental hospitals because she would lose herself in trance and not be able to get out. Sometimes she'd be out for days, and sometimes she'd just snap out of it. I don't know if you'd call it mental illness or just losing control of your spiritual self, but she would be hospitalized. We had to go to court to keep from being taken out of the home.

"My sister and I were always close. I took care of her. I felt like I took care of my mother, too, because she was operating on this other plane. So it was my job to hold the family together. Not that I did it well. I'd cook, clean, do things my mother wasn't dealing with at the time.

"My grandmother had taught me how to cook. She taught me to make kites, play the piano and the mandolin. She gave me reading lessons so by the time I got to the second grade, I was way ahead. Part of what she gave me in those years was inspiration as an artist. She gave me the foundation, and some things I still hold onto. When I go to school, I'm excited to go. And school was what kept me around in those years.

"I wasn't a good student, because there was so much going on. I just went inward. I tried to keep up with my art, and go to museums. But I didn't know how to build up barriers, so I isolated.

"My sister started using heroin. That's part of what killed her. She started real young. By the time she was 20, she had gone into a program. When she came out, she wasn't taking heroin or cocaine, but she was drinking a lot. I started drinking by the time I was 17. My sister was very angry, as I am, but her anger was more intense and directed at herself. By the time she was 30, she had pancreatitis, but she still continued to drink and drug. Eventually, each organ just started to shut down. So, by the time she was 40, two years ago, she passed away. It was a slow and painful death.

"Nikole, her daughter, was dealing with her mother's illness from the time she was three years old. By the time she came to live with me, she was whacked. The last two years have been about trying to get her back. Now, she goes to school every day. She has stability, and she doesn't have to take care of anybody. It's hard, because my mother, who lives with us, is sick, and it reminds Nikole of the whole thing. She does some really crazy things sometimes.

"She was grounded for all but two weeks last summer because she stayed out all night once, and because she was in a major fight up in another neighborhood and came back with a black eye. Packs of boys were in front of the house and the landlord had to talk to me and say, 'Either you've got to move, or get rid of these guys who are coming around in packs.' I mean it's like wolves. I'm glad she's wearing the uniform out in the street. At least they'll know she's in Catholic school and she couldn't be older, unless she was a

Leota with her niece, Nikole on the street in front of their Brooklyn apartment

complete imbecile, than 18. She's only 15.

"I told her, 'There's no maternity section in the Gap.' She likes Gap clothes. 'So, think about that. You're not going to be out there styling with Gap clothes, you know.' By the time I got her she was so different from my daughter, who wanted me to be there every second with her and she wouldn't go out.

"I finished high school and went to City College for a year. I was supposed to go to the School of Visual Arts, and I didn't have the money. That was a pipe dream. I got married by the time I was 19 or 20. I had my daughter by the time I was 21. I was married for nine years. I'd always known I was a lesbian, but I wasn't even near ready to deal with being both Indian, and a lesbian.

"I was 27 or 28 when I came out, and I came flying out of the doors. I left my husband. It wasn't working anyway. He started to change at some point. He wanted to reconcile. And that scared me. I thought, 'This might work. Let me out of here.' He wanted to reconcile. And I probably would have reconciled if I hadn't known I was dying in not living up to who I am.

"I remember before I came out I used to go to Central Park and there were women's softball games on Sunday. I was like the cavalry, or the Indians circling the cavalry. I was thinking, 'Oh, wow, these are dykes!' And I heard them mention bars and stuff. When I finally came out, I met a couple of women and they told me about an organization that was then called Salsa Soul Sister. It was third world women, and so I went down there. From then on I was really out there in the community. I didn't find too many Indians at all.

"I was really involved in my identity as a lesbian and lesbian mother. I took my daughter to different things. I joined this organization Dykes and Tykes and brought her down there and they had picnics and different forums about kids.

"Davida, my daughter — we call her Beanie — left home when she went to college. When she graduated, she moved to California for about a year and a half, then got her own place in Brooklyn not too far away. She took me out to dinner with some friends of mine on Friday for my birthday.

"My mom came back to live with me shortly after I left my husband. She stayed with me for three years, but it was too much for me, taking care of her and my daughter in two rooms. It reminded me of the hotel and I said, 'I just can't do this.'

"So my mom went to stay with my sister who vented her rage on her. I'm sure it was horrible.

"I started finding my identity as an Indian in the early seventies. It was simultaneous with my coming out, but I came out more as a lesbian than I did as an Indian. Then in the mid-eighties, I went to the Community House. Here in New York, since there are not a lot of Indians, when you come to the Community House, and you're willing to work, they grab right onto you.

"I volunteered for a lot of things there. I worked there, and I felt like I was home. I felt like I had found people who really understood, who had lived the life I had lived. I met people like Muriel from Spiderwoman Theater, who had mothers like mine. I said, 'My mom's a psychic.' And they said, 'Yeah, we know.' I said, 'So you know how it is.' We didn't even have to really talk about it.

"Part of the problem, growing up, was that we weren't in our community. If we had been in our community, we would have been taken care of in a way that we weren't. We should have had people looking out for us the way I'm an auntie now to some of the little kids who are in our community. Who cares for you and who watches out for you and takes an interest in you does not have boundaries.

"I say to Nikole, 'You've lived in secret, so you think nobody else is going to know about what you do.' I said, 'Everybody in our community cares about you. Nothing's going to be a secret. What you do, the women are going to know. And they're going to talk to you.'

"I don't want secrets. And I don't want her to think she can go and do something and it's not going to be addressed. Because all of us are vital to that community. It's not about what I do, it's about what we do. What I do affects the we. That's one of the things I have to learn when I'm applying for scholarships. I have to talk about *I*. And I'm not used to talking about *I*, because it's *we*. That's the only reason I've gotten to the point where I am, because of the community.

"Since I did not have my mother as a support, nor my sister because she was unavailable, I sought family in the lesbian community. Beyond that, I feel more family with — I was going to say the women in the Native community here in New York — but a lot of the guys there have been my family. It doesn't matter what their sexual orientation is. We all know things about the human condition because we're human. But the special thing about them is that they are Indian.

"I've been feeling that understanding in other places. I guess that's the good side of family. Because family has also been chaotic, secret,

Leota assembles the stretcher bars for her next painting.

distance, pain, not wanting to answer the phone because family meant disaster. I'm reconnecting with family because it has been so torn apart, especially my father's side. I found out the reason we were traveling back and forth was that it was part of the relocation program to get the Indians off the reservation during the Eisenhower Administration. Get them to jobs in the cities, which they were not ready for. My father wasn't ready to leave the reservation.

"People have been removed. My grandmother tells me one of her brothers was shot when he answered the door because he was an Indian. She had eight children. So many of them are gone. They've disappeared. My mother's never seen one of her brothers and another sister.

"I don't know what past tradition would say about who we're obligated to, except that I would say from what I see now, and it probably was true then, that we're obligated to the entire community. Not just your father or your mother. We're brought up with the idea that it's we, the whole, all of us, with respect, of course, given to those who have given birth to you, because everybody is dependent on each one that we all be whole and healthy, for the community to be healthy.

"There's one young woman I know who may be coming East, leaving her family. I said to her, 'Your family is who you make it, at this point in society.' I feel that, particularly if you are not what's supposed to be — if you're a lesbian, or if you're nonwhite — your families are struggling. There's nothing that supports the institution of family if you are any of these people.

"We have to garner our support from people who are not blood relations. I still can't totally call my mother family. I don't feel she was supportive of me. I don't feel she is supportive of me now. But I find that the director at the Community House is supportive of me. I'm acknowledged far beyond what I can even see of myself. Sometimes I have to step back and say, 'Who are they looking at?'

"I'm dealing with alcohol a lot, particularly behind my sister passing. I've recently made the commitment that alcohol is out for me. I've always talked about how devastating alcohol is to our community. I can't preach about it. Winona LaDuke talks about this historic grief we have. The escape is from the pain. The escape was from this family. I don't know what stops people from drinking. But I think part of it is the esteem that we don't have. I see so many talented people in our community that can't make that leap to say, 'Okay, here I am. We have to stop it right away.'

"We have to stop right away because of the deaths. I think of my sister, and wonder how can you get beyond a person's self-hatred? How can you get beyond the anger? When I would go out of this apartment to go get a drink, it was because of the pain and the anger. How do you stop it?

"It's very painful that I can stop drinking and my sister couldn't. But her kids can. I'm sure Nikole and her brother, who stayed with me a couple of years, are going to be okay. When he first got here, he's was wearing baggy pants and all these gangster clothes. And now he's with the drum group and he's working as a health representative.

"It's not like he came and said, 'Oh, wow, I'm Indian.' He's dealing with all the stuff that goes on in the Native community, being not full blood, not enrolled, not raised on the reservation. But he was saved from the streets. He was selling drugs, so he has a record. He could have, at that point, gone all the way out, or saved himself, and he chose the other.

"I've always felt hope in even the darkest moments. There is that little spark there is in all of us, I believe, and if you keep blowing on it, you'll liven it. I wasn't safe from starting and getting involved in drugs and alcohol. But there was something that kept me from going the route of my sister. I want to be part of our history and our ancestors. I'm an ancestor. I will be an ancestor. And I want to contribute."

A LOVE STRONGER THAN DEATH

ALAN AND WENDÉLL LA SHA
Los Angeles, California

Sometimes, when a man is dying, his family will gather themselves tightly around him, as though they could, through some miracle of grace and will, twist their love into a lifeline so strong, he will be allowed to stay. This requires a certain kind of man; he must still believe in miracles.

Sometimes, a man loves another man so much, his beloved is the whole world. Other worlds shrink away, and gradually family too – after all, who do you want to be there as your strong body slips away into the night and betrays you day after day? If it's not the smell of vomit, it's diarrhea and then a sweet, sickly smell from your own lungs and these are things you would spare your loved ones, if you could, except that one, except that one man.

Alan La Sha lay dying the day we came to see him. He knew it and we knew it, and Wendell, his partner of ten years, the man with the kilowatt smile and strong arms, knew it too. There were others in their family, many others they had loved, but here at the end death stripped them bare. They had lived life together, and now faced this together too, each man what the other had always needed.

ALAN LA SHA

46, retired educator and AIDS program administrator

"My father was my favorite person in the whole world. He was hard. He was not easy. But as I grew to see what he was trying to accomplish and build, I understood more. What my father taught me about being an African-American man is that there is nothing more important than my family, present and historical. Family, particularly from his side, was ancestral and remarkable. It was rich and historically rich. My mother's family was poor but proud. There was pride and honor in those families. It was a set of personal attributes about

where you came from and you never forgot.

"I found out after my father died that my ex-wife had told him I'd had an affair with a man. He couldn't talk about it. I was really pleased that he knew and still loved me. My one regret is that I didn't have children. I regret I didn't adopt. But I wanted everything to be perfect. I could have done it, but it took me until I was in my 30's to find out that life never gets perfect. And then, I was sick and I didn't think that was fair to the child.

"I have an aunt I really like. She's very strong, almost 90 and very sarcastic, and I respect her. I have a brother who I don't like and whom I don't feel close to. I have severed the relationship at his request. I have cousins and about 25 other people, a tremendous back-up of friends who are family to me. Friends are what family's all about — people you can count on, who would do anything for me and for Wendéll. It's incredible to have so many. Most people are lucky if they have one or two. At the same time, someone said to me, 'No, you're not lucky. You have worked a lifetime to make these relationships.' It's true and I'm really proud of it. I realize if I have any good in me, and have anything to offer society, it's probably that I know how to connect with people.

"Particularly since I've become ill, Wendéll and me and our little kitty have a family unit that is ours alone that doesn't belong to anyone else and no one else will ever belong to it. It's funny to include the animal, but he's bonded to us. Most of my time is spent in bed when Wendéll is gone. I get very tired just sitting in a chair, and when I'm in bed, my cat is there. He's up against me and he fights to be next to me and I know it's protective. He didn't used to be that way.

Alan and Wendéll La Sha.

Alan spends most of his time with the cat, watching television or sleeping.

"Wendéll and I have had experiences together because I've been sick that you can't have with a friend. Other people probably would clean up my vomit, but I'm not comfortable with it. Wendéll does it and he doesn't complain and he looks at me and says, 'You'd do it for me. What am I supposed to do?' We have a very loving, special relationship, as much as we get on each other's nerves. There are times when I just want to slap him, but he and I have a very unique, just-the-two-of-us relationship.

"He has always loved me. Even when I tried to get rid of him, and did get rid of him for about eight months, he refused to step out of my life. I told him we were just going to be friends, and he said, 'Fine. But I'm going to be there for you.' He believes when you love someone, you don't

disappear. Then he moved, but I had to move right with him. Even when we argue and have difficult times, I know he loves me. You can look at him and see it.

"My family is the center of my life the way it was the center of my father's life. My relationship with Wendéll is the most important thing in my life, period. I feel very blessed by that.

"Unless there is a miracle, I'm going to die. I'm not afraid of it. I was in the hospital earlier this year and I was dying and the only thing that made any difference was Wendéll. The only thing. Friends, money, nothing. We have difficulties accepting that, but he's turned out to be a lot stronger than I thought he would. He gives me what I need in terms of realizing this is going to happen and that it hurts me. I'm doing the best I can, for and with him. It's difficult to talk about, but this is uniting us even closer. This phase of our lives is ours.

"As gay people and particularly as African-Americans who are still dealing with the concept of being gay African-Americans, we don't always remember that there are a lot of us out there, who lead very private lives, and who are very proud of who we are. We all fight different battles, and we all do it in different ways, so we aren't always

immediately visible, but there are people who will carry on the struggle.

"For those African-American gay people who have a dream of having a gay or lesbian family, you really have to go to a greater level of maturity than people go to in straight relationships. A lot of society is going to knock you and criticize you. Even our own community makes it difficult. The AIDS crisis is helping us, but we haven't learned to accept the fact that we are families and we have to support each other. It's work, work, work, ten times more work than straight relationships. But it's worth it, because it gives us something to grab onto and believe in. And it shows us in our hearts and our heads that we can be bigger. We can meet those challenges. We can have a relationship against all the barriers people put up."

WENDÉLL DOYLE LA SHA

39, supervisor at health maintenance organization

"We met through mutual friends. Alan had the reputation of being the person everyone wanted to date. He was attractive and learned, seemed secure and in control. But I was never drawn to Alan because of how attractive he was. There's a side of Alan people don't know, which is very insecure. And that's the side I fell in love with. Actually, I didn't find him interesting until we started talking.

"When I came out at 16, it was difficult. My father and brother had the hardest time. Being the males, they didn't want a faggot in the family. But every family has at least one. It got to the point where I blew up and the house emptied out and when everyone came back three or four hours later, the approach to me was different. From that point on, I think everyone said, 'Well, we don't like

Wendéll helps Alan get up from the couch.

this, but we're going to have to accept it.'

"I was raised in South-Central Los Angeles and my family was very close when I was growing up. I'm closer to my father now than I was when I was younger. He depends on me a lot now. When I was younger I think he thought I wasn't going to amount to anything. But now, he's proud of me, and he looks up to me because of my knowledge of certain things.

"When I was growing up, family meant we supported each other. That's why I'm so close to my sister. When I wouldn't take up for myself, she would. And I've been there for her, too. When I was growing up, in South-Central, before the Watts riots, the sense of family meant protection and warmth. It was very important to be part of one. In school, when I met a child who had only one parent, I couldn't imagine our family not having both parents. I didn't particularly care for the way my father was, but I couldn't think of not having him there. It was very important to me to be really close to both my parents and my siblings. I've tried to be close to my brother, but he just doesn't have it in him. The sexuality is not the problem; he's just one of those kind of men who can't say they love you.

"Alan and I have been together for ten years now. I wanted to get married; I always wanted to be a black June Cleaver. When I realized I was gay, I wanted the same thing that a lot of females want: to get married, have a home. And to a certain degree, I got it. We're limited now. I wanted to travel the world with him. I wanted to go to Europe and do certain things with him I knew I wasn't going to do with anyone else. It makes me angry sometimes.

Wendéll talks about growing up in Los Angeles.

"What I love best about Alan is his sense of humor. He has a wonderful one and I don't. I'm serious about things I shouldn't be serious about, and I've made things hard for myself. With Alan, I've learned to laugh. He keeps me focused and he keeps me from falling. I can finally look at myself and I learned how to do that through him. He gives me direction and balance. There are things I wouldn't have tried if I hadn't been with him. He's

brushed some of my insecurities away and in some ways, I have helped him do the same. We balance each other out, basically. There are some times when he truly works the last stitch in my nerves, but we've worked it out.

"When he's gone, I'm going to continue to live with his spirit. We've created a bond that death won't break. This is marriage to me in the fullest sense."

[Alan La Sha died on January 16, 1995. He was surrounded by his family and he was not in pain.]

SAVING THE FARM

BARTON HEAPS' FAMILY
Glen Rock, Pennsylvania

Rita Mae Brown's poem "Sappho's Revenge" claims: "An army of lovers cannot fail." In rural southeastern Pennsylvania today, there is a small army of ex-lovers and lovers and friends who have gathered together since April of 1994 in an effort to save their homestead, which is Barton Heaps' farm.

Directions to the farm include landmarks like billboard signs and stores on a two-lane blacktop about an hour outside of Baltimore, Maryland. For over ten years, certain lesbians from Baltimore, Washington, D.C., and points in between have come to Barton's farm twice a year, Thanksgiving and July 4th, for gatherings that have become ritual and familial. The food is bountiful, as is the peace and quiet. Birds sing here and tomatoes grow healthy and huge in the back garden. A brook passes in front of the centuries-old farm house, and the stones of an old spring house tumble down beside the path over the brook bridge to the house.

Barton has been an active member of her community as a printer and print organizer for more than thirty years. She was part of the collective that published the feminist journal, *Women: A Journal for Liberation*, in the sixties and seventies, and she has printed most things that have mattered in the Baltimore lesbian community since then. She never made any money, of course, and her hands are still stained with ink. These days, she's had to move the press into the farmhouse; she didn't have enough money to keep a storefront shop going. And she may lose the farm altogether, if the tax man gets his way.

This is not an unfamiliar story in rural America today. But the ways her family has chosen to stick by her may be unfamiliar to many Americans. Barton's family is the best kind of army, and they are fighting for her and for the home she has made theirs.

BARTON HEAPS
58, printer

"I've lived here in Glen Rock for 23 years. I was living in Mount Vernon, outside of Washington, DC, but the woman I was lovers with then, Franci, wanted to have horses, so we decided to get a place in the country. We had a couple of friends in this area; there was an ad for this place in the Sunday paper. It was only the second place we looked at. It was perfect.

"At that point, things were a lot less expensive than they are now. We scraped together enough money for a down payment, although none of us had a penny at that point, which seems not to have changed a bit.

"We bought it in 1971. A year later, Franci split to go to Vermont with another lover, but I decided

Left to right on the porch of the farmhouse are Janet Bardzik, Anita McCurley, Alice Aldrich, Barton Heaps, Dean Birch, Lucky Sweeny, Jan Braumiller, Frances Heaps, and Deborah Vitkovah.

Barton loads a metal plate onto one of her small offset presses in the basement.

THIS PRESS WAS MADE POSSIBLE
WITH THE SUPPORT OF
Lee Lally
Jack Engeman   Maureen Fahey
Inez & Jerry Fenster   Anne List
Peggy Harriz   Maureen McGuire

Every year, we have a Fourth of July party where 40 or so women come, and we have 20 or so women on Thanksgiving. Those parties have become tradition — they've been happening for eight or ten years now. For myself, I like the fireworks. I go back to being a child. I also like the company who comes.

"This home means safety to me. My mother is buried here. If I have to leave here — I try not to think about this, but — if I have to leave here, I find it very difficult to come up with an answer about where I would go.

"Alice and Dean, my sister Fran, Jan and Deb — these are women I can be frank and truthful with. I can say, 'Hey, I've done this stupid thing.' I was embarrassed, but I needed help so I swallowed my pride and went to them with these troubles. I needed $2500 almost overnight, and they got it for me.

"The whole community has given me an amazing response, with the fund raisers and all. I think of myself as out here on the farm, doing my thing — I dip into the city and print *Women's Express*, which is a monthly publication for women out here. The message I'm getting is that the farm means a lot more to them than I ever realized. It's been just an overwhelming feeling of love and gratitude and amazement."

ALICE ALDRICH
49, physician's assistant

"When I came out, in Washington, D.C. when I was 27, I wanted family desperately. Family meant people were there for the holidays. Some of my most horrendous memories are when everyone would go home for Thanksgiving, and I would be

to stay here and keep the farm. Up until this point I've basically done that. The farm is paid off but it's not going to be for long.

"I was not trying to evade taxes, but I haven't paid any kind of taxes for a long while. Years ago, I had an accountant who said, 'Hey, if you're not making any money, don't worry about it, because by the time they catch you it will be a wash anyway.' I've always been running behind and I figured I wasn't making any money. I'm more of a printer than a bookkeeper anyway. I stuff envelopes in drawers, that crazy kind of stuff.

"They say I owe an enormous amount of money. In December I started opening the envelopes and realized it was serious. Then my younger sister Fran started helping out with the accounting and in April I finally got a tax lawyer. I'm trying to sell two acres of the property, and see if I can get refinancing. If I can't get a new mortgage, then the greater part of the farm will have to go for sale. That's the part that really hurts.

"This place is my home. It's part of who I am. In a larger sense, it has to do with the community.

alone because my birth family and I had gone our separate ways. People would go home and have miserable times and come back and want me to put them back together again.

"My life smoothed out when I got into recovery. Barton and I became lovers and I stayed at a job for more than a year, that sort of thing. In a sense, some of my recovering community felt like family. We supported each other through the holidays. It was a place that was safe, where you didn't have to play-act. But there was a transitoriness to it. I feel like I have created family with Barton. I don't think we set out to create that situation. I think we fell into a place where we just did the same things over and over. One morning we woke up and said, 'You know, this is kind of nice.'

"There are people who come to Thanksgiving and July 4th whom I have known for twenty years. We've been pissed off at each other, gone through a lot of emotions together, which I think is something that happens in families where you're allowed to be something other than just a happy face. And you look around one day and realize some people have been there in all the crucial places, like the day you move in the middle of the week. And some of these people I'm not all that close to even after many years, but if they didn't come to Thanksgiving, I'd feel bereft.

"I think what it comes down to is that I want to be seen and known. I want people to know who I am and what I think and feel. I want to be as weird as I want to be and still be accepted. To be in a family means you don't have to have the mask.

"And I do want some people to go through my whole life with me. I don't want my life to be a series of monogamous relationships and friendships. When I'm 80 I want people to say, 'You know, I've known her for 50 years.'

"What I've seen happening in our community is that people are choosing to stick by each other when we don't have to. We're not bound by a legal document. At any point, any one of us could get up and walk. We don't have to stick around and help Barton salvage the farm. We are choosing to because she's important to us and we love her and I can't imagine doing anything else.

"I feel fiercely about this place. I come out here

Alice and Barton, former partners, are still very important to each other.

and spend idyllic moments on the front porch with my coffee, watching the birds. It's quiet and beautiful and it feeds my soul. For years I would come out here and tank up on the peacefulness. It's not something you can get in the city.

"Barton is a very accepting person and she's not territorial. So people have come here and put their stamp on it, fixed something or planted a plant, whatever they wanted to do.

"You can never say exactly why you love someone and I don't think you can say that about what works here. And even though Barton and I are no longer lovers, we are going on as family. There isn't a name for our relationship; I used to say 'Barton and I are lovers, but not lover-lovers.' Now I say we're kin. My new lovers have to understand that I will continue to put time and energy into Barton."

FRANCES HEAPS

52, bookkeeper

"Barton and I were not close as children. It was a very strange family situation. My mother and father were living with my grandmother at the time I was born. My father was an alcoholic and a gambler and didn't support anyone. My mother and grandmother supported the family, but my mother was an alcoholic too. So for all intents and purposes, my grandmother took me as her own and I was estranged from most of my direct family.

"Barton was my hero as a child. We had a connection, being abused by the same man, one of my mother's lovers. But when I came out at age 14, when I walked into my first lesbian bar, Barton was sitting there and just about fell off her chair. For years I was known in the community as Barton's

Dean clears a trail of tree limbs which have fallen during a recent heavy storm.

little sister. It was pretty annoying.

"But since I was younger, I moved in different circles. I drank. I was an alcoholic and Barton was not. She was in fairly monogamous relationships and I was being really crazy, and more and more I just moved away from my birth family.

"I began to do serious incest work. It took me a long time to realize how furious I was with Barton. I had an expectation that she could have defended me, or protected me from the abuse. It took me a long time to a) realize the rage was present, b) tell Barton about it, and c) let go of it. I stopped

drinking about ten years ago, with some relapses. I've been totally sober for about eight years. Once that was past, I could look at things more clearly. My mother died, and that made it easier to give up all of the rage and turmoil inside of me and get closer to Barton.

"I've known for a long time that financially Barton wasn't doing well. I didn't have an inkling of how bad it was until she called me and told me the tax authorities were after her and that she might lose the farm. As a bookkeeper, I just said, 'Oh shit, Barton.'

"She doesn't, and I don't, have the money to hire an accountant to help us. So we're just going to have to put things together and figure out how to keep the farm. My contribution is that I do the books. And I'm trying to train Barton to pay attention to this now so she doesn't lose control of her life. I don't want her to feel as though she can't do any of this. For both of us, as incest survivors, not feeling like a victim is very important.

"Sometimes I stand back and I look at Barton, and it just astounds and delights me that Barton is so connected to this community and, more closely, with this smaller group of people. It's like a figure eight, this river of family that she has gathered through the area.

"One example: This house has been really run-down. So some of us organized a painting week-end. There were 30 women up here one weekend. We scraped, primed, and painted the whole house that weekend. A woman volunteered to cook and women were camping out and sleeping all over the house. Most of the women who came were about twenty years younger than the rest of us. It felt as if this spirit of community and the spirit of this farm was moving on to the next generation. When they left, the farm was shiny white, and now they are organizing another weekend to fix the porch.

"A large part of the reason this happens is Barton. She is the spirit of this farm – her gentleness and her openness. Barton walked down a path that these women are contemplating walking and it's now paved because of Barton. She really did something with her life. She doesn't know it. I don't think she has any clue of the love and respect that people have for her. I don't think if she really sat down and thought about it she'd

understand why either, and it's very difficult for her to take it in. Now, thirty years later, being Barton's little sister is a point of pride; it's no longer a thorn in my side."

JAN BRAUMULLER
44, artist and Spanish teacher

"In recent years, Alice has encouraged me in my art work. Also, I know I can call and ask advice of her. She will listen and give me an honest answer.

"I've given Barton a sum of money so she could retain a lawyer to fight for the farm. The farm is integral to the sense of family I have with Barton and Alice. The holiday rituals have always been at Barton's farm, and similar celebrations in my own birth family were very important times of being together. In the case of Thanksgiving, it was at my aunt's farm. So Barton's farm relates to good memories with my birth family too. I've wanted to live in the country full-time for a long time. This is a place of retreat for me, and I know I can come here and pitch my tent and just listen to the birds when I need to."

DEBORAH VITKOVA
46, photographer and teacher

"Alice was one of my role models in recovery. She went first. Over the years, we had fights and found out we couldn't travel together, but we still stuck it out. Alice and I were the women most overt about our anger in all of Washington. Except for Jan, who's been inflicted with me daily for eleven years, no one knows me better and has accepted me more honestly in all my monstrous incarnations than Alice has."

Frances and Barton Heaps visit the site of their mother's grave on a hill behind the farm house.

LUCKY SWEENY

47, astrologer

"I know Alice from a group we were in for a number of years; that started about 15 years ago. I've known Barton even longer, from Waverly, a leftist, political neighborhood in Baltimore where we, and lots of gay men and lesbians, lived in the late sixties. It seemed so adventuresome and exciting to all of us when she bought the farm.

"Family certainly means the biological unit into

which one was born, a classical definition. Past that, it is a term I don't particularly like; it brings to mind attachments that are empty. I've seen so much crap done in the name of family that it doesn't have any pleasant connotations for me. When I think of my extended group of people, I think of them more like a tribe, or steal Vonnegut's idea of 'karass,' from *Cat's Cradle*, which is a group of people you are born into at this time, who may be related to you or not, but are part of some vibrational unit. Also, another idea is Aldous Huxley's 'mutual adoption society' in *The Island*, his utopian novel. He has the community live in groups of mutual adoption, and people, when they are having trouble with their families, go to another family unit. They are in a committed family relationship with each other for life. And that feels true for me with some of the women here. These are the people I share 90% of my life with, as opposed to my biological family, where I share only 10%.

"One of my closest friends, who happened to be a cousin, was killed in a car accident a few years ago. It was a great tragedy for me. I'd always thought we would grow old together, and that's what I think of when I think of family: forever people. I'd love to find other models that weren't called family."

JANET BARDZIK

41, respiratory therapist

"Most of these women are in some sort of recovery and most of my family is not. So the women here are dependable in a way that my biological family is not. This is a peer family and comes from a history of oppression. These

elements of recovery and shared experience create an inherent trust, so I feel valued and safe within them. If I weren't a lesbian, I wouldn't have this family of choice. And there's nothing in the world to compare to it."

ANITA McCURLEY

49, personnel classification analyst

"It's been very upsetting to me to think that Barton might lose the farm. My immediate reaction was, 'Oh no! What if we can't have Thanksgiving?'"

Lucky Sweeny and Vicki Phillips evaluate a purchase. Plant sales will help meet the Federal tax obligation.

And then I thought, 'It can happen somewhere else, but it won't be the same.' So about eight of us produced a dance. We raised around $1,000. We had a country-western lesbian dance, had lessons, a dee-jay. It was so much fun!

"Family can be another lesbian who I never even met before, but I recognize as being connected that way. Family can be the people I hold near and dear

Anita McCurley relates a story to Alice Aldrich.

through distance and time: the living, the dead, and all the animals who comfort us in between. I used to think when somebody died, 'Oh, that's it,' until I learned that you keep loving them and they keep being part of your life.

"A wonderful woman, Louise, who was a mentor to me, died of breast cancer. She's in my heart and she's still alive for me. There was a gay

man who was my travel agent, who died of AIDS. I grieved for him, but then I realized, if there was anyone I wanted to go before me, it was him. When it is my time, I'm going to say, 'Wayne, I want a direct flight and no stop-overs. Please make arrangements for me!'"

WALKING AWAY FROM EVERYTHING... INTO LIFE

MARCIA KAWAHARA'S FAMILY
Los Angeles, California

It's one of those weekend mornings in L.A. when almost anyone would want to live here. You can see the San Gabriel Mountains in the distance, and freeway traffic is light. Jean and I park on a wide residential street lined with blue-collar versions of Better Homes and Gardens entryways.

The house is set back from the street and surrounded by bushes; the driveway curves to the front door, and Marcia welcomes us in. She introduces her partner Mary, her daughter Lani, her sister Andrea, and Andrea's husband, John. There will be a time for interviews and photos, but now we sit down to a brunch of eggs, bagels with cream cheese and peaches, and fresh orange juice. The eclectic cuisine of this melting pot city is very California. Some of us have our orange juice with champagne and some of us do not. And bagels with peaches? Different.

Conversation with breakfast is relaxed and warm. These folks are easy to be with. While the dishes are being cleared and the interview space is being prepared, Marcia spreads the newspaper across the table. Mary and Lani shop the furniture ads and slide the comics over to John. Andrea admires a hand-carved acorn squash, and I get out my camera as a house cat rubs up against my leg.

MARCIA KAWAHARA

55, social worker

"I think, from the time I was about 16, when I had my first really big crush on a woman, I knew I was a lesbian. But I didn't even know the word then. And I certainly didn't use it after I saw it in literature. I did a real effective job of denying everything, and going on with what I was programmed to do.

"Even though I'm a third generation Asian-American, there's still the programming that you marry, you have children, you are the cornerstone of the family. You are to stay home and be the epitome of a feminine ideal. You are to serve your children and your partner. Even though my parents were Nisei, which means they were born here in this country, and they had lived a very American lifestyle, and we were raised in that lifestyle, the cultural carry-overs are very great.

"So, I married a very kind and gentle man I met in college and we were together for almost 25 years. He's very atypical for a Japanese man. In some ways he was more of a feminist than I was. He started the first girl's basketball team for his high school on Kauai, and coached them all those years. He was a great advocate for women in sports.

"Then I saw 'Desert Hearts' in New York. I discovered that Jane Rule had written a book. And when I got back to Kauai, I found out the publisher, Naiad Press, and had the bookstore get that book for me. When it came in, I saw on the back the list of other Naiad titles. I started sending for all the books Naiad published. That was the only company I knew of that published literature about lesbians. A lot of it was pulp. There were also a couple of other interesting things: anthologies and books about real lives. That was my exposure to the gay world, period.

"I went to the point of getting myself a post office box so I could receive this contraband. And I read it in privacy. I did this for three years or so. I realized this was what I had been all my life. I had never been attracted to a man, really. What I think attracted me to my husband was his goodness. I'd never really thought much about physical things. But then, I realized that whenever it came to a woman that I basically developed a crush on, it was physical.

"I had these great desires. When I finally read about other people like this, there was no other conclusion I could come to. And when I came to that conclusion, there's no other action I could have taken.

"I told my husband first. He knew I had been troubled. I was drinking a lot, and I isolated

Left to right, Lani Kawahara, Mary Wynn, Marcia Kawahara, John Marshall, and Andrea Spolidon

Andrea asks Marcia for the serving spoon.

myself. He guessed on the third try what it was. He said, 'Well, I know that you really like to be with women.' When I would meet someone professionally, I'd get very involved, and develop friendships. And those were only with women. I didn't think he'd even had any clue.

"He said, 'Do you have to leave?' And I said, 'This is all about being honest. This is about finally living an honest life.'

"He said, 'It's okay. We can work this out. You can do your thing, and still be with me.'

"I said, 'No. Haven't you heard me?'

"I was in shock. I thought, 'Well, I'll just have to go. And I'll have no job, no money, no home.' It took me about a month to get off the island. During that time, I came to my senses and explored ways to get an extended leave from work, because I was in emotional crisis. I told them, 'I'm going to the mainland for therapy.' Which was part of it.

"I announced to my sister that I was in big trouble. 'I can't tell you on the phone,' I told her. She came on the next plane. I was semi-hysterical. It took me the longest time just to get it out. I couldn't tell her at the airport. I had to wait until we were in our hotel room. And I told her this long story about how everything led up to this. I said, '"Sister, I have to tell you that I think I'm a gay person.'

"I'll never forget the way her face kind of dropped. She said, 'Is that all? Not that I am diminishing this in any way, but I thought you were going to commit suicide. Or you had cancer.'

"'This,' she said, 'we can deal with. This, we can handle.' And she proceeded to help me in my coming out process.

"The moment she got back to Los Angeles, she talked to friends of hers who are gay and lesbian and found out where to go for information for me. She went to the Connexus offices and sent me all their literature. She went to the Gay & Lesbian Community Service Center. She met Yolanda Retter, who was Director of Lesbian Central then. And made an appointment for the two of us to see her when I arrived.

"I was just astonished, because of all of those years of self-hatred and contempt for myself and guilt. To have someone say, 'Hey, I love you anyway, I love you first of all,' was the most affirming thing. It was like a second chance at life for me.

"My coming out was really an accelerated process. I just did everything. I learned real fast, too. By the time I met Mary, I'd had four affairs. But with her, the sparks didn't fly. I thought she'd be a good, solid friend. You know, she'd be a nice person to hang out with. And she thought the same thing about me.

"We started getting physical about the third time we were out. And it was just really nice, you know. After that, it was boom! I thought, 'Whew, I think I'm in love with this person.' And it was the same thing for her.

"But, it was slow. She couldn't let anything happen until she trusted me. She has a long history of betrayal. Finally she realized that truly with me what you see is what you get. One thing that she thought was very positive was that unlike people she'd known before, or she'd had relationships with, I had had a very long and successful one.

"Having a ritual or commitment ceremony doesn't mean that much to either of us. The things that do have value for me are the tangible things. It shouldn't be that I can't extend my health insurance to cover her. She has this chronic illness. I feel badly that we're in this kind of situation.

"At the beginning I was totally convinced that I was the only Asian lesbian in the entire world, because my only exposure to the lesbian world was through books. There was not a single Asian person in any of those. I must have read 80 books. All I knew at that time was the white lesbian experience. So, when I came to Los Angeles, and I became involved with a group of Asian lesbians, it was a real eye-opener for me. But they were all very young. It's still the case now.

"When I went to an Asian lesbian retreat, I met Crystal Jang. She was out in the 60's, and that just really blows me away. She's wonderful. She's a mental health professional, and she was at an Asian community conference on mental health. Somebody brought up the question, 'What about Asian homosexuals?' And the facilitator, another mental health professional, said, 'Oh, there aren't any Asian homosexuals.' This made her get up and say something. And she has been out ever since, and very visible. She's Chinese. Other than her, I don't have any role models.

"I came here, and I thought, 'Well, I'm going to be a bag lady. But I'm going to be a bag lady in a gay area. At least I will be with my sisters.' I knew it would be hard. You have images of what a lesbian looks like, and how a lesbian acts. I am as far from that as anything I knew of. I dreamed about finding a partner, and I worked hard at it when I got here. But that wasn't the most impor-

Andrea shows Lani a carved acorn squash, a form of edible artwork done by a Thai man in her Asian elders program.

tant thing to me. The most important thing was being able to live every day honestly. And I thought I'd die if I couldn't do that, if I didn't give myself that chance. I was never a full, total person until I did this. I never would have imagined the positive response that I've gotten from practically everywhere – from family to friends, to the workplace. I feel completely integrated. I have never felt so free or happy in all my life."

ANDREA SPOLIDORO

50, Associate Director of
Asian Pacific Older Adults Task Force

"Marcia called me in 1989. She had had a very hard series of years preceding that. I thought, in all of my naivete, that she was going through menopause. And she was. Physically, she was going through menopause. Emotionally, she was going through so much more that was dangerous to her, because it was not embracing of her. She couldn't be herself.

"She started calling a couple of years earlier and saying things like: she felt she was a phony, that frogs were coming out of her mouth every time she spoke. She said, nobody really knew her innermost self, and, if they did, they really would reject her.

"I thought, oh, god, hormones totally out of balance. And I flew back there one time after a phone call, and just appeared at her work, and said, we've got to talk about this.

"About a year and a half later, she called again, and it was worse. She said, "I'm sorry, I have to go away and never see anybody again." I put down the phone, and thought, 'God, something's terribly wrong.' It was at a critical stage in my work. So, it took me about five days to delegate everything. John put me on a plane, and I met her in Honolulu. I was really shaken up, because I felt she was desperate.

"We went back to the hotel, and she said, 'I'm a lesbian.' For a minute, I got totally angry. I said, 'Is that it? I have been out of my head with worry

about you for five days, and that's it?'

"I said, 'Honey, that ain't nothing. What did you think this would do?'

"She said, 'I thought you would reject me.'

"I couldn't fathom why she thought this would be so horrendous. I said, 'You're not alone. You're just like a whole lot of other people I know. We'll just deal with it.'

"So I took her to a lesbian club in Honolulu. Drove down there and let her loose, and went back to the hotel and waited for her. We talked about it. I stayed with her for two weeks. We went back to our island. She said, 'I'm going to have to leave.' And I said, 'Okay. Let's start planning.'

"There's no anonymity in Kapa'a, Kauai. There is no way of hiding or keeping something private. Marcia and I have 76 first cousins. We come from an enormous clan. Our grandfather emigrated from Okinawa, and was the leader of the Japanese community on our tiny island.

"When I first got married, I was 20 years old and I married an Italian. My grandfather flew up here, and said a prayer over my head in Japanese. Later, I asked my uncle, 'What did he say?'

"He said, 'You can never go back home again. You can't come back to the island.'

"I was the first female in the family to marry outside my race. They would have stoned Marcia to death, figuratively, for being a lesbian.

"It's not easy for gay people in that culture. At some levels, they are extremely accepting, such as of cross-dressing. If you are a male in Hawaii, you can go to high school in full dress with make up. The lesbians and the gays on that island, on the surface, are accepted due to *ohana*, the cultural idea of family. But underneath, there are vicious jokes.

There is lack of understanding.

"*Ohana* is your connection with people, whether you're related to them or not. You live on that island and there are families there. And you belong to one of the families. You are identified that way. You are the daughter of so and so, the sister-in-law of so and so, the cousin of so and so, the mother of so and so.

"*Ohana* is a spiritual idea. The closest uncles I have are two calabash uncles. They're not blood related. But they took care of me growing up, and I love them. They're in my *ohana*. They're in my family. A person becomes part of the *ohana* by living there and being invited places, and being loyal and taking care of everybody, and contributing.

"The family is extended, inclusive, open, welcoming. But also, it lays down the law. There was no way Marcia could stay there, because she started off in a position of social power, as a social worker, as a member of an *ohana*, in a family, as a wife, a mother, a friend. For her to switch and say, 'I'm a lesbian,' it would be like she said, 'I'm a fraud. All this time, I was a fraud. And you didn't have to give me your love and support, open your homes to me. You didn't have to because lesbians aren't accepted that way.

"The *ohana* comes together in *luaus*. They talk stories. They have community festivals. Their whole lives are intertwined. And they're seen as travelling in their *ohanas*. Everybody knows the four who went golfing, who drank, who did service, who were professionals, whose children are going up to the mainland to college, who every Christmas went to Honolulu to buy gifts. And Marcia said, 'I'm not that.'

"When she told her friends she was a lesbian,

they said, 'You'll get over this.' Now, she maintains communication with them, but not as close as before. The one closest to her was the one who said, 'I love you anyway.' The other two made judgments. And they're not in my *ohana*, because they made those judgments

"After I took Marcia to the lesbian bar in Honolulu, we went home and decided how she would leave, what she would pack, and what she couldn't pack. I flew back up here after two weeks.

"I sent her huge packages of stuff. I knew she was in pain. She thought she was the only old lesbian in the world. She thought she was the only Asian lesbian in the world. She had no idea about the world.

"She had so much she had hidden for so long. And it made her feel so alone. And she needed to find out so much very quickly.

"When she arrived up here, about a month later, we had a ball. I used to drive her to women's groups, and sit out in the car and wait for her. John and I sat up waiting for her after the first dance she went to. She came home raging drunk and happiest I have ever seen her, because people came up and asked her to dance.

"We went through so much. We went through tokenism. Some people wanted to see her because she was Asian. And then she met Mary. Poor Sister, what an economic catastrophe. Finally, after living with us for three months, and getting her own apartment, moving again to be closer to work, she got a full time job. She figured she had to get herself settled, so she bought a beautiful little condo here in Pasadena. Six weeks later, she meets Mary. Eight months later, she's living with Mary. She had bought furniture, cost her thousands of dollars. She had to move all that furniture out, give it to Lani. She took a bath. But she was very happy.

"Mary is a healthy person, who's had some very traumatic experiences. But in some ways, she, too, was so lonely, and was at the point of giving up finding something.

"And I kept telling Sister, 'You know, you look and you look and you look. But the minute you stop looking, you're going to run right into somebody.' And that's exactly what happened. It was great.

"I love Mary. I love the fact that she's very dedicated and protective and loving of my sister. She has changed on account of loving my sister. She's kind of like John in a lot of ways. They've both got things driving them that are very deep and very dark. And so, when they come across people like me and my sister, they hang on. Because we're not part of that darkness. They're both extremely smart about relationships. They're willing to take risks.

"To people who are uncomfortable with their gay brothers and sisters, I would say, 'Please just let go of some of that fear. If you're afraid that much, then it must rule your life. No one can do anything to you that's going to make you ineffective and a nobody.' If I knocked people out of my family because of that, I don't know what I would stand for. I don't know what would satisfy me. There's nothing out there that's that scary, really."

MARY WYNN
48, professor

"Our relationship has certainly made me much more sensitive to cultural issues. Now, when I go to a lesbian function, I'm very aware of the ethnic make up of the group. And, more often than not, it's either all white, or there'll be two or three people of color there. I'm uncomfortable with that now, myself.

"When I see Marcia being discriminated against it makes me very uncomfortable and angry. Last summer, we decided to buy some property. The realtor would not look at Marcia. She would only deal with me. I don't think the woman even knew that she was doing it.

"It was difficult, because we had other friends with us who worked with this woman for a long time. We debated whether to stay with her. Marcia said, well, she was only going to buy a house from her, she wasn't going to sleep with her

– or something to that effect. But I was still uncomfortable and angry, so we decided to stop dealing with her.

"I can't imagine not being with Marcia. Even though we are only four years into the relationship, it feels long term.

"I like that Marcia is very animated, and very up most of the time. I tend to be more serious, so we balance each other nicely that way. But the thing I like best is her caring and warmth. There's no pretense whatsoever about her. I feel I know exactly where we are and what's happening all the time."

LANI KAWAHARA
28, student

"I was already going to school in California when my mom came over here. She didn't tell me why she had left at all. She just said she was going to die if she stayed in Hawaii. She told me she and my dad were divorcing. First I didn't believe it. Then I was angry, because I didn't know what she was doing. She wanted to tell me, and I just didn't want her to tell me yet because I wanted to get through finals. It was my last quarter in college.

"I think I actually found out before. She was staying at my Auntie Andy's, and I had gone to get something from the room. And she had a book on lesbians or gays. So, I kind of put two and two together. So, I waited a little while after that to let that sink in. I felt this was probably going to be it, and that would be okay.

"When she finally told me, it was a relief. The way she had been saying she was going to die, and that there was no way she could live on Kauai anymore. I wondered, 'What? Is she sick? Did she

kill somebody?'

"When I was in high school, I dealt with it because my dad was a basketball coach, and I played on the girls' basketball team. People assume that if you're on a basketball team that you're a lesbian or something.

"I think my dad is happy as long as my mom's happy. My brother doesn't talk too much about it.

"I like Mary. But it's something new. When she first knew Mary, we started different traditions. As Mom put it, it's the same type of family, but a different form. There's a lot of affection in this family anyway. So, I think it was easier to deal with, even if it was two women, touching and kissing and stuff.

"Mary and Mom work well together. My mom has an angel sitting on her shoulder. She could go through life and not notice important things that she should be doing, but in the end, she'll get where she's supposed to be. She floats around sometimes. And Mary is easygoing and very logical and practical. She's down to earth.

"There's nothing I regret about my mom's identity. I'd never seen how strong she could be until she came over here and left everything there, just brought what she had, and started a whole, brand new life without even being sure that's what it was. When she came over here, she was really scared. I'd never seen her so scared before. After she figured out what she was doing, I've never seen her so sure, either."

Left, Marcia and Mary smooch while grilling chicken.
Above, Marcia and Lani play with their dog, Amy.

IN JESSE'S BACKYARD

MICHAEL PHILLIPS AND ROGER RUSSELL
North Carolina

If a woman's hairdresser is a man, he may be straight – or, if the woman lives in the South and is a white woman of a certain class and a certain age, he may be the only gay person she knows. If she likes him, that woman could go to him once a week, or once a month, or whenever she needs him, until they can't remember how many years have gone by. He becomes treasured by her and she becomes special to him, and they share a bond that neither takes lightly.

Let's say that man is generous and giving. Let's say that woman has married a man who becomes too sick to work and so finally she takes a job in a mall. Let's say she's still proud, even though she has little money left. The hairdresser knows this, because he knows most things about her: He knows that her daughter is a lesbian when she has told no one else; he knows when she hasn't been sleeping; he knows, literally, what has turned her hair white. He knows exactly when to be silent and how to help her when she can't accept help.

Let's say that for a short while this includes doing her hair for free. He doesn't need the money now anyway – the man who has been his lover for almost thirty years has done well by them, helping him run the salon, and investing the profits in real estate. Let's say he never says a word about this to anyone. But she remembers even though years

pass. And because of the culture they live in, she still knows almost nothing about his life and knows no way to thank him.

Michael Phillips is that hairdresser. The mother of a close friend of mine is that woman.

Michael lives quietly in suburban North Carolina with his partner Roger Russell. Michael is active internationally in his field; he and Roger have good friends both at home and abroad. Like many gay folk, they are not 'out' to their biological families or at work, but they have been accepted as a couple by both sides of the family; Michael's family 'adopted' Roger one year. This is how things are done in parts of the world where words cannot be spoken, but where good people find ways to be good people even when the law of the land wraps the strictures of silence around their hearts like chains.

MICHAEL JOSEPH PHILLIPS
49, cosmetologist, educator and business owner

"My mother named me for two characters out of the Bible, being the good Baptist minister's wife she was. Michael was the archangel of God, and Joseph, of course, wore the coat of many colors. My heritage on my father's side was Crow Indian. My people lived on a *mill-hill*. They were the poor who worked in the mills around here. I've always

been working class and I like to identify with people who made a contribution, with givers.

"Roger and I have been together for 26 years. We met in a gay bar. After our first date, I left my watch behind so he'd have reason to call me, because I liked him a lot. I still like him a lot. When he's in the yard, the birds will come down and follow him around–he's that kind of person. There's no doubt we'll be together for the rest of our lives.

"Early on, we decided we wanted that kind of relationship. We used to tease each other about the vine-covered cottage, but after a few years, we had one. We wondered how it happened, but I think respect had a lot to do with it. When we first met, I was real immature. Roger is older than me, and I needed, and wanted, to learn a lot from him. The first part of our relationship was about him teaching and me learning. But there came a time when I realized I wasn't there because I needed him anymore, but because I wanted to be with him.

"It happened one night when we were getting ready to go out, and the steps were icy. We were coming down the steps and he got me by the elbow and was holding onto the railing. Even now, it chokes me up because I realized he really did care for me; he didn't want me to fall. That made a real impression on me. All those things I had held back left me in that one minute. I knew this was it. From

Michael Phillips and Roger Russell horse around in front of their North Carolina home

then on, I was there because I wanted to be.

"We've always gotten teased – we'd come in and people would say, 'Oh where've they been – to the prayer meeting?' because Roger and I have always had a monogamous relationship. Almost every night, before disco when people quit talking, we used to go out to be together. We were identified as a couple and no one ever bothered us.

"Family for me is having someone you can count on, emotionally, and for all of those things you need to be whole. Roger is the better half of me. He's so precious to me and the longer we're together, the more I feel that way. I watch him from a distance and look at his pretty little head, and I still think he's wonderful. I know this sounds sentimental and I hate that I'm going to say it, but I'm as good as I can be because he's been there for me. I don't think I would have reached as many goals as I have without him.

"The relationship with family is one where people aren't ashamed or embarrassed by you. My mother has gotten older, and she's got Alzheimer's. She'll spill her stuff, but I don't get embarrassed anymore. It's more like: Let's get this stuff cleaned up.

"Family is in the heart. You have to have that core to be able to take chances and not experience ridicule (or nothing permanent anyway), so that you can go out into the world and be the best that you can be. It's that solid ground that supports you throughout your life. I think that's why God made families anyway. It's that nurturing protection so that you can grow.

"We've been fortunate enough to have a real close relationship with our real families. Roger's sister would introduce me as her son and so would

Michael does the hair of Catherine Swallow, the author's mother.

his mother. They used to call me Becky's other boy. I'm real proud of that.

"I am concerned about how we're buried. People don't have to know that we were lovers, but I want his name on my tombstone, and vice versa. I want that for our history, and I want it for gay history, too. A hundred years from now, I want people to know that we meant something to each other, so much so that we put it in stone to show it.

"Right now, at the salon, I'm more open than I was previously because of my age. Everyone there now knows that I'm gay — and we're all real close. Sometimes we're together twelve hours a day. It's like living together!

"I have a real varied clientele. Some people's hair I've been doing for 33 years, and I'm already doing second and third generation. I'm old! See, I've been doing hair since I was 16. But I continue my education, and I do progressive work, so I have a lot of young clients, too. When you cut someone's hair for a long time, you can come to love them. With some, I've watched the progression of children, and the conversations about them, and I take all that to heart. I listen, and if there's anything I feel like I can say, I do, but mostly I listen. I listen to the turmoil, and I admire some of my clients, when they have the courage to face their lives.

"I've always thought that being gay was something special. I can look at things from both sides. But I've had a hard time reconciling my religious upbringing with what I could glean for myself personally. I just try to keep it as simple for myself as I can. I thank God for what I get on a daily basis. I don't take even the drive to work for granted. I still enjoy watching the trees and the seasons and appreciate them for being there and

me for being here.

"I do talk about Roger all the time with my clients; I can't make a sentence about myself without mentioning his name. But as far as when our anniversary is, I don't share that, or the little sweet things that happen."

ROGER LAMAR RUSSELL

56, real estate management

"Probably, I was fourteen years old when I realized I liked boys better than girls. It scared me. I was the youngest of eleven children, raised in a family of macho boys who all played sports, but I played in the band, which I was teased about. When I was fourteen, I had girlfriends, but I realized I had a boyfriend too. I knew we weren't supposed to be that close, but I think he felt the same way. It wasn't a real sexual thing, but we both got scared and we never talked about it. We drifted apart, and I've often wondered about him.

"One day, when I was in my early thirties, I just decided that I needed to come to terms with myself, and I went to a gay bar. I went a number of times before I met some people I was interested in; I was never interested in casual sex. When I finally saw Michael, he was tall and slender, with beautiful hair, and I was immediately struck by him. We went to some friends' house and he left his watch. I took it to him the very next day.

"I was ready to decide who I was and what I wanted, and I think Michael was too, even though he was younger. Michael has a wonderful sense of adventure, and he was very enthusiastic about everything. I was a big talker, and he liked my stories. We were genuinely friends, something outside just the sexual. I had always thought that

was a necessity. And I think I knew at the time I wanted to spend the rest of my life with him.

"I liked having a partner. I never thought of it in terms of a traditional marriage – that makes me think of preachers and religion, things that are alien to me. At that time, we weren't allowed to think of ourselves as married; we thought of ourselves as committed, a lifetime commitment. We've made a partnership based on a lot of trust and mutual commitment. I can tell you, I've never had an outside sexual relationship, male or female, and I don't think Michael has either. That's the one thing I think is required. It has to be totally monogamous.

"It has to do with respect, too. I've always thought of Michael as an equal. In the early years, I may have been the more dominant force, but one of the things that I think I've done for Mike is to give him

the confidence to be equal. I've pushed him to take responsibility for some things he used to leave up to me. People ask about our age difference, but I don't think it's ever really affected us. Once Michael became more confident, he was able to take on with more comfort more leadership in the relationship, and more of the business of the salon.

"It hasn't all been a bed of roses, like any relationship. You have to work, work, work. All the things that make people different made us different – Michael was brought up in a very strict environment, and I was brought up in a very permissive environment, for example – but I think the differences are what made us work.

"We have families, and I think that's probably one thing that holds us together. They always acknowledge us, and we're lucky with that, but we made that happen, too. Michael told my mother

and my older sister who lived with my mother, that they were his refuge, where he could come in the door, take his shoes off, lie down on the couch and take a nap. He said he felt more comfortable in her house than he was at home. Of course that made her feel good, and it made me feel good.

"Every Sunday we were in town we went to my family's house and either took them out to lunch or they fixed lunch for us. Then we took them shopping or took them for a ride. I missed having that close relationship with his parents. But his father was preaching then. In her own way, I think his mother did the best she could to accept us.

"We set out to create, consciously, a family. His nieces and nephews have said to me they can't remember a time when Michael and I were not together. And several of my nieces and nephews have said the same. I take a lot of pride in the fact that we have been able to create a bond with both families.

"His family 'adopted' me. Michael's mother and daddy were going through a painful experience with his dad's church, so Mike and I went to them. We spent lots of time with them, trying to help them through the crisis emotionally, financially. We got them moved, got new curtains put up, things like that. So that Christmas, they adopted me. I think it was a way of thanking us. Several of Michael's brothers knew what we had done, and I think it was their idea. It was a total surprise to me. We were having Christmas dinner, with all the grandchildren, and they brought out this document they had handwritten. It was the next best thing to saying we were okay and they understood. What they did say was they just realized I was a member of the family anyway, and they wanted me to know that even though they didn't have a legal way to

Roger holds forth in his home office about his family roots and civil war history.

make me a part of the family.

"We wanted to set an example for some of the younger people in our families coming along. They have told us they do see us as role models. And now, I don't think they could ever have a negative view of a gay person.

"It's unfortunate that this religious element controls so much of our political and social lives. I don't really know how to deal with bigots. It's like they say, 'Don't confuse me with the facts; my mind's made up.' You never make a dent with them. I don't waste my time. Jesse Helms is a total embarrassment to me, North Carolina, and the human race.

"I'm a happy person, and I think Mike and I have had a happy relationship. I've been very fortunate. Mike teases me that I don't ever want anything. But I feel lucky in my life. I'm a whole person. I've got good friends, good family and Michael. We've been able to make some contributions and I think we'll leave a good legacy. I really think our families are proud of us. Who could want anything else?"

THE LIMITS OF LANGUAGE

IRENA KLEPFISZ'S FAMILY
Brooklyn, New York

Geoff and I are spending the morning with Irena Klepfisz in this third-floor walk-up studio she shares with her long-time partner, Judy Waterman. We have walked across the Brooklyn Bridge earlier and I am awake, for once, at nine a.m. Irena is letting Geoff use her computer to fax a letter that can't wait. Geoff is accomplished in these things, and he is teaching her how to use programs she has never seen before. I am sitting in a chair next to the bed they are working on, and I am watching them to see who she is.

In the computer lesson, many words are repeated out loud, including Irena's online name. The Yiddish words she chose seem to me to perfectly describe her life: one is a word for family, the other, for immigration. In 1943, Irena Klepfisz's father smuggled her and her mother out of the Warsaw Ghetto; he stayed and died a hero's death in the Uprising. Irena and her mother lived by passing as Poles, but Irena spent part of the war in an orphanage, unable to see her mother who worked as a maid. After the war, Rose Klepfisz took her daughter to Sweden, where they stayed until they eventually made their way to the United States. Almost all of Irena's extended family perished in the Holocaust.

It is difficult for Rose to talk about that time. Even now, fifty years later, she grants no interviews

so she will not have to answer questions about it. I repeat Irena's words softly to myself, thinking of the good barley soup Rose fed us for dinner the night before, a gift exchange for the refused interview. I look out the window by the bed, and I think about Judy, sitting in the light from that window's twin at the other end of the studio, so solitary yet so close. And I think again how families cannot be killed even when people are. Even when our families don't 'qualify' as families by the limits of language, even when we wish to avoid being in families, we seem to make them anyway no matter what we call them. We make them in all the ways we make soup, and partake of them in the same necessary way.

IRENA KLEPFISZ

53, teacher, activist and writer

"I've always felt an outsider; I don't think I ever got over being an immigrant. I never dressed right; I was definitely the greenhorn in the neighborhood. It's kind of ironic because before we came to the States, we lived in Sweden for three years. I was the only Jew in my school, and the Swedes were very wonderful to me, very accepting. But when I came here, I came to a predominately Jewish neighborhood, working-class immigrants, and I was a total outsider. None of it guaranteed

me the feeling of home.

"My mother was very upset when I came out. She felt it wasn't safe. And she had her own sense of what she wanted me to be — to get married and have children. I think she got flak from her friends. For her generation, fitting in was very important. And it was also very difficult for her that I would not have children. It's an issue that doesn't go away. I had always assumed I would have children, even though I never married. I don't know what I thought would happen. When I came out, lesbians weren't having children. In fact, it was politically wrong to have children then. There seemed to be no way for me to make that happen. Then, when I was 39, I had a hysterectomy, so it made it impossible. But it's a sore point for me. I'm the last living member of my father's family, and it's very painful for me. Sometimes I have deep regrets, often when I'm confronted with death.

"Knowing I'm the last of the line is a terrible feeling and it's visceral. But on the other hand, intellectually, I hate this whole blood mystique. There's a part of me that finds it politically abhorrent; I hate the word 'family.' There's a way in which I hate it because I lost so much family in the Holocaust. The word 'family' itself feels painful. I never had my family; I can't even remember my father. I was one and a half the last

Irena squints into her computer and hugs her cat, Yossin.

Judy Waterman, Irena Klepfisz, and Rose Klepfisz.

During the photographic session there is a disagreement, an uneasy peace, and then a joke breaks the tension.

time I saw him, and I've had a number of surrogate fathers. But I never had a family. A family was defined for me as at least three people and not two people and we were two people.

"I always felt the absence of my father. But it was also the absence of my aunts, my grandparents, the whole large extended family. Even if I'd had a grandmother, that would have been something. But it was just the two of us – my mother and me – and that did not seem to count in other people's eyes. With seders for example, I could never say we were inviting the family to the house. That makes the person who doesn't have a family feel as though she were lacking or less or abnormal.

"I think the way people use the word 'family' in this country says that human beings only have value when they're connected by blood, and that you would do more for someone who is connected to you by blood. I really object to that philosophically. I understand strong emotional ties, but there's something about people who find out they're related when they haven't known each other for 40 years and suddenly that relationship is supposed to take precedence over other people they've known for the last 20 years. It's very exclusive.

"Politically, what happens in this country is that they say, 'Your family should take care of you; government shouldn't take care of you; the responsibility is the family's.' I think that encourages people not to be responsible for each other. Family becomes the reason for not doing for someone else. And of course, most of that responsibility will come down on one woman.

"I'm very ambivalent about family. Part of me wants it, and part of me rejects and is angry about it. The whole concept has caused me pain, because

Irena admires the sweaters her mother knitted for the adopted child of a cousin.

it's made me feel I'm only a remnant of something. But, I was very taken with the idea of having Judy and my mother and me in one picture. They both hate to be photographed. And it became more intense for me when my mother got sick. I don't know whether the word is family, but these are the most significant women in my life. And I wanted a visualization of that, because they don't want to talk about being a family.

"Judy and my mother are the constants in my life. Judy probably knows me better than anyone else. She understands my sense of isolation. She

And I imagine always being with her. I can't imagine leaving New York without her.

"Now about my mother – well. What I love most about her is that she can be a very funny lady. She can be very loyal, very fierce. When her stubbornness is not directed at me, I like her stubbornness. And she's a real survivor too; she's very gutsy. It's amazing what she's done with her life and what she's achieved. She's very decent and cares about doing things right. 'Decent' is an old-fashioned word, but it means that you treat people honorably in some way; you don't do dirt to people.

"I do think she's proud of me. One time she said to me, 'You know Irena, you really did a lot and you didn't do it the easy way.' She'll wax poetic with other people, but with me, she's not so open, so that was a great gift. I'll take her to the library and punch my name into the computer and then print out whatever comes up and she really loves it. One time, at a ceremony honoring my father, she said that one of the last things my father told her was if we survived, he wanted me to have a good education. She's very proud of my doctorate.

"My mother and I have had a very intense relationship. She was my only family for years, and my center. And that was both good and problematic as I got older. She's my sense of continuity with the past; she's the link. And she's been very present in my life. This is a woman I generally talk to every day and now more so since she's been sick. I don't know what I'm going to do when she's gone. I find it very frightening. I know it's going to happen at some point, but I can't even imagine it. I'm hoping it won't happen for a long time."

understands me as an artist, and a lot as a Jew, though she's not Jewish. She's someone with whom I share a very similar view of life. And we care about each other a lot. We protect each other. It's a very deep, complicated relationship we don't talk about or label. In some ways, it works better for us to not label it. It gives us an illusion of freedom that in fact we don't feel. I don't think either of us feels like we can just walk out.

"One of the things I love most about her, and it's something I remember from the first time I met her, is how she laughs. She is one of the most somber people with one of the most hilarious laughs I know. And Judy really taught me about art. She was much more developed than I was when we met. I was all instinct then. And she always points me back to my writing. She anchors me in a very important way. She taught me not to listen to the audience; she just paints and doesn't allow it to stop her if no one sees her paintings. And her work has always been very moving to me.

"She's one of the smartest people I know and she drives me crazy sometimes. We're both extremely obsessive, which is a disastrous combination. But we're really different too; it took me a long time to learn that she became a painter because she doesn't like words so much! She's a survivor in certain ways, and she's very gutsy. She's one of the most complicated people I know.

"In some ways, the relationship is changing without us talking about it. I think we're closer than we've ever been. I think we're much more accepting of our differences and able to let each other alone in a way we didn't fifteen years ago.

JUDY WATERMAN

57, artist

"I met Irena in 1975; we have a mutual friend who introduced us. That year, both Irena and I had gotten grants from the New York State Council on the Arts. I had just read Irena's book (*Periods of Stress*) and really liked it, and I was having a show of my paintings at a downtown gallery. Janet, this friend of ours, knew I liked the book, and she wanted Irena to see my paintings. So one day, while we were walking and Irena was driving by, Janet literally flagged her down. We ended up driving down to the gallery and Irena saw my paintings and it was a very nice way to meet.

"I was always drawn to Irena, but I knew her for some time while she was living with another

woman in Park Slope, and I saw them socially with other friends. About a year later, Irena and I got involved with each other. It has been a very intense relationship. When we moved in together early on, it was very difficult because our personalities are so different. She goes through periods where she's very expansive and sociable, and I tend to be very withdrawn. I like a great deal of quiet and peacefulness. But I think that's partly how we were drawn together too. She tends to keep things stirred up, and to some extent, I enjoy that, although it can become overwhelming.

"I'm never bored with her. I'd rather be alone than be bored in the presence of anyone. I'm very drawn to her intelligence and her humor. We have talked easily about art and creative process. There are a lot of good reasons for being with her, and not a lot of good reasons for not being there.

"It's been 17 years now. There was a period of about six years when we didn't live together, but we were always in touch, aside from one period of time when I was living in the country and wouldn't answer the phone. I don't know if we'll always be in touch, but I want to be.

"I do think of Irena as family. I don't want to seem to be too enthusiastic. It isn't easy for me to talk about this, or any relationship. 'Family' is not my favorite word. I had very ambivalent relationships early on, so feeling committed in any way has always been really threatening to me. Feeling like I'm making some kind of final or permanent move is frightening. I'm not a settler. I can't characterize my relationship with Irena very well. There's something wrong with the language about family, about partnership, about relationship, about all of it.

"What I find odd about the idea that gay people don't have families is that people think that's a criticism. Family isn't anything I've wanted to cultivate. There's something absurd and peculiar to me about wanting to replicate the experience of family, which was a kind of torture for me. I think lesbians talk about family a lot because they don't want to be excluded. But I think it's healthy to be excluded from the conventional family. I want to say, 'Girls, it wasn't that great.'

"But obviously, people gather others around them, somehow, and whether they are related through heredity or not is irrelevant. There will always be groupings of close people. So whether we call it family, or don't, whether it has the respect of the conservatives or not, doesn't mean anything to me."

CHOOSING A LIFE

GORDON SMYTH'S FAMILY
San Francisco, California and Portland, Oregon

Gordon Smyth retired early. At 63, he stunned employees and physicians at the large medical practice he had successfully managed for 12 years. He came back from his annual horseback retreat into the wilderness mountains of eastern Oregon and said essentially, "Take this job and shove it." Now he does outreach to isolated senior gay men in Marin County, California, conducting small groups. Raising hell and consciousness everywhere he goes, he speaks out about what it means to be old, gay and male. When he got up at the annual national American Society of Aging meeting and "came out" as an old man who was gay, the old lesbians cheered and whistled for him. He cried when the support washed over him.

He is a man unafraid to cry. Full of dignity and a passion for justice, he is also unashamed. When he was a young boy, and teased by the rougher members of his family, his Aunt Gladys spoke out for him, saying, "It's a poor family indeed that can't afford one gentleman." His family today stretches from Seattle, where he was the son of an Irish longshoreman and his native Washingtonian wife, to Portland, where he cultivated artists and patrons for the region's best craft/art gallery, to San Francisco, where he was one of the nation's first "chocolatiers," importing chocolate from Europe for uninitiated American palates. Posted on his

Gordon Smyth.

refrigerator are not receipts or grocery lists, but a line of Russian poetry: "In the morning, therefore, I am not frightened that I have chosen to live a life unlike that of other young men."

GORDON SMYTH

64, medical management consultant and outreach worker to senior gay men

"I've reached a point in my life where things have sifted out and what remains is very important. I don't see people who are tangentially important anymore. I just don't have time. The people here have sorted themselves out and have become an integral part of my life. I suppose the common thread with all of them is the spiritual quality of the connection we share.

"I remember saying to my mother at a very young age when we were on our way to visit relatives, 'One of the problems with family is that you feel an obligation to be with them even when you don't like them. The wonderful thing is to be able to choose your friends.' Now I'm in a position where I've chosen not only my friends, but my family. The difference between friends, and friends that have been absorbed into family, is the level of our communication. It doesn't happen overnight. We have to work at it. You know you've reached family when the other person is as willing to work at it as you are. It's wonderful to realize when someone cares enough about you to want to get through the kinds of obstacles we so often put in the way. It's stunning to me when someone cares enough to make that happen. When you leave the world behind, and stop giving each other weather reports, you can do some serious stuff.

"I am single, but I don't feel alone at all.

"Someone who's not here is James, the love of my life, who was nearly the death of me. I will never forget meeting Jimmy. Of course he knew I was watching him. How could he not notice my eyes hanging off my shoulders? I picked him up that night and never let go. I fell desperately in love with him. When I think what a fool I was, how addlepated! I loved his physicality, and he had a spiritual quality about him which even then was very clear. He wrote poems to me, and drew pictures that were really – well, we were in love. You only get one of those I think – no, you get as many as you want, but you only want one if you've had one. One is enough.

"He died in November of 1993. I'd lost him as a lover a long time before, but never as my love. When Joanie and I drove up for the memorial service, there were continually rainbows the whole way up to Seattle. Everywhere I turned, there was a rainbow. I kept thinking, 'That must be James, that must be James,' because rainbows were such a part of his personal iconography. Joanie thought so, too. So now when I see a rainbow, I think, 'Hi, James, how're you doing?' It's just like he's there. I think about him all the time.

"It's so awful to see all these men dying. I told James this before he left. I feel such a sense of abandonment. James, and Greg, and how many of

my hairburners – these people are supposed to be here, and they're not here. If Waz goes, I don't know what I'll do. I really don't know what I'll do. It's awful. But I'm still here, and he's still here, and Jean, you're still here. And it's our job to take care of each other and to stay healthy."

WAZ THOMAS

50, program coordinator and yoga instructor

"I've known Gordon about fifteen years now. I've always had effortless rapport with him. We disagree on things and are very different people, but we find each other interesting and funny. Plus, he's an excellent cook. He cooked all the time when we lived together. I was totally happy to walk into the kitchen and eat his food. He was very supportive of me when I was exploring my art, which is rare. People think of family as people they like to be around and share lots of experience, with but I thrive on a great deal of time by myself. Gordon understood that immediately.

"People call themselves family when they're in very destructive, malfunctioning relationships. The word itself doesn't have any value. If I ever need anything or anyone, Gordon would be right there, and I think I would be there for him. I can't imagine not being friends with him. When we're able to be physically together, which is not that frequently now, we just sort of take up where we left off. The passage of time is irrelevant to the deeper spiritual connection. That's something Gordon and I have never talked about but I suspect that the quality of our relationship comes from a spiritual connection that I can't really define.

"Now I'm out there on the edge, with my HIV positiveness. Without romanticizing, this is, in many

Above, Gordon's San Francisco family. Left to right, standing, Peter Goetz, Gordon Smyth, Kathleen Crane, and seated, Jean Swallow. Right, Gordon's Portland family, left to right, Jean Swallow (just visiting), Joanie Campf, Gordon Smyth, and Ron Crosier. The three empty plates are set for the photographer and two older lesbians who feel they need to remain anonymous.

Gordon takes a walk by the ocean with his long-time friend and former lover, Waz Thomas.

ways, the best time of my life. Gordon and I haven't talked about it much. It will unfold as it unfolds."

PETER GOETZ

*42, psychotherapist, administrator of
AIDS psychiatric program*

"I met Gordon through Waz, but I didn't really get to know him until we went on a spelunking expedition in 1981. Gordon is now one of my best friends. He's definitely part of my family, although we've never discussed that, nor do we need to. We talk about being men together, not necessarily being gay men, though we talk about that too. And that talk has a real matter-of-fact way about it. We both have the desire and the capacity to be campy at times, but also to be authentic with each other.

"The way a lot of gay men and lesbians come out in the world is very alienating. For many of us, building families of linkage and connection is very healing. It's important for us to feel that love and connection because it's the antithesis of the alienation of homophobia. It's important for us to say, 'This is the innermost circle.'"

JEAN SWALLOW

41, writer and editor

"I met Gordon seven years ago at a medical management meeting where he said something very cogent in a situation that was designed for obfuscation. His remarks were clear, direct and somehow dignified everyone there. I, on the other hand, was so enraged by the condescension of the meeting organizers I could barely speak. When the meeting was over, I chased him down the hall and asked him to lunch, which was quite bold given his and my relative positions in the hierarchy, but he

knew how to do something I didn't, and I wanted him to teach me. Since then, he has taught me more than I ever knew how to ask for, and over time, we became best friends. He says now I was his teacher, but this is an extremely generous assessment of the situation.

"Gordon possesses a generosity of spirit that is, in my experience, very unusual. This generosity extends towards all living creatures and becomes a kind of respect. For the longest time, I thought he knew everything and that was why I felt so safe with him. Today I know that's not true. He doesn't know everything. But he knows the greatest thing of all: He knows how to love unconditionally.

"And he has loved me that way. I asked him to be my best man at my wedding and he walked me down the aisle. During the service, I was laughing at something and I turned to him, as I usually did, to share the laughter. He leaned over and whispered, 'You're having entirely too good a time,' and I saw that he was crying and laughing at the same time. I realized suddenly how hard it was going to be for him to let me go live my life in another state without him, but there he was, helping me go. In that moment, I knew what it was like to be truly loved. It was the most wonderful wedding gift I got, and the best teaching he has ever given me.

"He has sanctified my life by his love. This is the gift of real families."

JOANIE CAMPF

51, owner of advertising business, writer

"I've known Gordon for almost 27 years. I met him in community theater. I think we just fell in love with each other about thirty seconds after saying hello. When I look at the pictures then I see

how young we were, and even then, he was joyful. One of the ways he would say hello to me was that he would take me by both my arms and look me in the eye, and I felt completely connected with him. He was not the kind of person who spoke with his eyes going by you. From the first time I met him, he was always emotionally available to me.

"Very soon after meeting Gordon, I had surgery, and Gordon and some other friends came up to see me. The four of them sat around in my room while

Gordon gets a hug from Jean while he mixes the dinner soup pot.

I was semi-conscious, just laughing their brains out. Finally they left and two hours later, I got a telegram from them. They were just having the best time in the world. The telegram said, 'Wish you were here.' It was so typically Gordon.

"The richness of our lives, even as we've changed, is that we've always been very present with each other. We go up into the mountains horsebacking every year, and last year we were both at some big crossroads. So we went up to the mountain and sang this song about going up to the mountains and not coming back in chains. And we would not allow the other person to come back in chains. That's been our power.

"He's tied to my spirit. He's my lover in a way that men and women don't often define, but is possible. He's that close inside me. The word friend is not sufficient because it doesn't have enough passion and compassion in it.

"Gordon has kept hold of me, even when I've let go of him. I love him for that. He's always said, 'Look who you are.' At the times when I thought I was nothing and no one, he's taken my eyes out of my head and put them into his and said 'Look.' And somehow, fixed in his head, I could believe it. That's an extraordinary gift. He would often give me back me.

"Up until a few months ago, family meant blood family to me, although I have always known that my friends are my strength. Now that I've lost my blood family, I recognize there was this space I kept between me and my friends. I carried with me an illusion of closeness of what my blood family represented to me. When that illusion was finally gone there was an emptiness inside me, and I wondered for a long time if I was going to have to fill that emptiness by finding a lover. But now, in a very formal way, I'm bringing others into that space that used to be filled with named family: parents and brothers and cousins and such. Now the people who are in there are of my heart. The space is now a sacred space.

"Blood families can, and do, hurt you deeply, because they are automatically in that space. It never occurred to me you could bring people into that space who would not damage you. But that's what I've done and it's the safest feeling I've ever had. It's not that the people I've brought in won't hurt me, but there's no intention of that. I'm very much more joyful and secure than ever.

"Gordon and I have sat on this floor on nights when I couldn't leave home, and celebrated Shabbat – this man who was raised as a Baptist and this woman who was raised as a Jew. We lit Shabbat candles and shared Sabbath prayers. Once when we were in the mountains, it happened to be Rosh Hashanah, and I said to Gordon, 'This is important to me. This is the Jewish New Year'. And

Joanie and Gordon kiss.

he said, 'Then we'll spend it that way.' So we went down to the river. I took my prayer book and we sat on a log that was out over the river. We looked up, and in front of us was this marble mountain with the sun splashing against it. The opening lines

Above, Joanie Campf tells a story to Ron Crosier.

of the prayer on Rosh Hashanah is, 'Hark, look ye to the mountains from whence you came.' There was not a moment I ever felt more connected to God, and what God wants out of the universe – that feeling, when a person took the time to say, 'I

am in this with you. This will be a new year.' And we sat on the log and made up prayers and read prayers. That's a family."

LOVE AT FIRST SIGHT

KEITH OCHELTREE AND CHARLES-GENE MCDANIEL
Chicago, Illinois

The day we arrive in Chicago, the weather is typically summer with muggy heat and blinding thunderstorms throughout the afternoon rush hour. Geoff and I have driven in without a city map, but the highways are undergoing repair and the route signs are either missing or invisible in the rain anyway. With new directions from an old man at a gas station where no one else would talk to us, we make our way to Lakeshore Drive, and from there, it is only a few blocks to the cool quiet of the apartment where Keith Ocheltree and Charles-Gene McDaniel have lived for over 20 years.

They have been partners since 1955, after meeting in a hotel lobby in Harrisburg, Pennsylvania. Gene takes us through gracious and well-proportioned rooms which are kept shaded from the afternoon sun, and he points out particular art works from the collection he and Keith have gathered over the years. The apartment has the feel of Paris: Large, old windows are open, but sound is muffled and the air remarkably cool, and calm. There is the feeling that wonderful conversation will happen in the still sophistication of that silence.

Keith is sitting in his chair in the front room and around him are amassed his reading materials, his walker, his cane, his writing board, things he might need and might not be able to get up and get. He has been ill for some time but his mind, and his

acerbic wit, are as bright at Gene's smile. Later, Gene will make dinner for him; although that is the reverse of their decades-old order. Keith largely stares straight ahead at the closed blinds of the windows, playing with his cane and occasionally thumping it for emphasis. He does not mince words. Gene does not hover over him; Keith is not a man over whom one could hover. But when they make their slow way down to the courtyard of their apartment to show us flowers, Gene holds back, guarding Keith, and when they sit down for a moment on a bench not unlike the bench on which they sat forty years ago, getting to know each other, Gene tenderly holds Keith's hand, and helps him rest.

CHARLES-GENE MCDANIEL
63, educator and writer

"I was working in York, having just moved to Pennsylvania after getting my Master's degree from Northwestern. Keith was working in Harrisburg on a state government project, classifying personnel on a merit system, which is his expertise. He has a Master's in Public Administration. I had come to Harrisburg to visit a school friend and was having lunch in a coffee shop. Keith sat down a couple of stools away from me. After lunch, I went upstairs to the hotel lobby and he followed. We sat and

Keith Ocheltree and Charles-Gene McDaniel in their midtown Chicago apartment.

Gene makes dinner for the both of them.

looked at each other. Then we walked across the street to a park, eyes following each other. We finally got to talking and found out we had a lot in common.

"I'm a Quaker. I had been a conscientious objector during the Korean War. He had been at Pendle Hill, a Quaker retreat I knew of. He was an intellectual, and had social concerns. Even though he was in the war, he was not a militant warrior. We both love music, we both read a lot – although he reads history and economics and theology and I read a lot of literature and psychology and science. We're both socialists and obviously quite liberal; we've both been involved in the civil rights movement. We talked for a long time and exchanged addresses that afternoon. He finally came to York to visit me, and the rest is history.

"I was head-over-heels immediately. I was looking for a partner and I was determined to have one. We were friends from the start. It was more than just chemistry, more than just biology. We had fantastic love-making and I adored him from the beginning.

"In the '50's, it was very oppressive and it's hard to recall on an emotional level what it was like because things have changed so much, but there was an edge to being gay then because of the danger. You could be arrested on the whim of any policeman. The bars were raided routinely and without provocation. You had no rights. You could be sent to a mental hospital, in addition to being sent to jail. And many people lost their jobs after being caught up in raids. Jokes were made. You were a faggot and a fairy and all kinds of assumptions were made about your life if they knew you were gay.

"I've never hidden the fact that I'm gay, although I haven't been able to be as open about it as I am now. It was pretty well known that I was gay, inside and outside the Associated Press where I worked for a number of years. But the AP was less judgmental and oppressive than other employers because there were other openly gay people when I was there. I was able to write gay-positive stories, but that was the exception for those times. Psychiatrists and psychologists said we were sick and this was very damaging to one's self-esteem and ego. It was a great burden to keep all this concealed.

"I think it was more of a burden for Keith than for me, because he's ten years older than I, and I've always been feistier. I didn't care what people thought about me, but there came a point where I had to put on a protective carapace, in order to keep from being hurt. Illinois was the first state in the union to decriminalize same-sex behavior, I think in 1962. In 1975, the American Psychological Association said that homosexuality was not an illness.

"It hasn't been easy. Being a Quaker and a socialist and gay – well, I was put on earth to make trouble. This started early, even in the fifth grade. I knew I was different early on. I was in high school before I was able to say that the difference was that I was gay. I had not had a serious relationship before I met Keith. I don't believe in God or any of that, but it was very strange that Keith and I met. I used to go up to New York before I met him, looking for a husband, and, of course, that's not the place to find one, but I had hope. I wanted permanency and we certainly have had that. We've been support and consolation for each other. He's disabled now, and we've had a tough time. He has arthritis in his spine. The summer before last he nearly died, and I nearly died as a consequence. He was in the hospital for 32 days with necrotizing pneumonia, and an abscess on the lung, in addition to the arthritis. He had to learn to walk and eat again. The year before that, he had congestive

heart failure. I'm having to face the inevitable and I don't like it. I've never known adult life without him and I don't know what's going to happen when I have to face that.

"We are certainly a family. For me, a family is two or more human beings who are voluntarily associated, who face life together, who are committed to each other and love each other unquestionably and unquestioningly. It doesn't mean a piece of paper that's paid for in the City Hall, nor a piece of paper signed by a member of the clergy.

"We're together because we want to be. We could walk out of it anytime, but we haven't wanted to. We don't disagree that much. There aren't many things worth disagreeing over. We may not always vote the same way, but we think so much alike. And we live simply. We don't have an answering machine or a fax. We have no air-conditioning and

no car. We're not obsessed with possessions and we have a rather cynical attitude about things that matter to many people. We think materialistic values are silly. Sometimes now I think I should have devoted myself to a little more material gain, but still, we'll manage okay.

"We take the Quaker approach. When the way opens, there is the answer. And if no way opens, then it's not the end of the world; you wait. Probably Keith gives in to me more than I give in to him, but on the other hand, I make concessions too, and without saying so. Now I've restricted my social life; even though he says, 'Go on out, go on out,' I feel uncomfortable doing that. I go out some, but mostly during the day, and I don't go away on trips for more than a week. My secretary, who's a lesbian, looks after him too, and will call him up to see if he needs anything.

"I don't give a damn whether someone thinks I'm married or not. For me, I'm married. And Keith is my partner, for life."

KEITH OCHELTREE

73, retired, formerly in public administration

"We've lived together since 1958; we met three years earlier. I had been wandering around the park in Harrisburg, waiting to be picked up to go down to Gettysburg. He was wandering too, killing time. We got to talking and I went off to Gettysburg to sightsee. A couple of weeks later I went down to visit him. I thought he was an attractive boy, nice. I wasn't looking for anything at that particular point. I wasn't cruising because it wasn't a particularly cruisy place.

"I thought we should get acquainted. I thought there might be something down the road. I stayed in

Harrisburg for another year, working, and went down to York most weekends, and now and then he came up to Harrisburg. In the summer of 1957, he came to Chicago to see me, and after that he was able to land a job here. He came and lived with me in my little studio until we could find a larger place, about three blocks west of here, where we lived for 15 years. We've lived here for twenty years.

"When I met him, I didn't think I'd spend my life with him. I don't think I looked that far ahead. I suppose I would call it a marriage. I guess that's what it is, really. We've never gone through any special ceremony or anything. All that's been long since our time. But it feels like a marriage; we're very much a part of each other's lives.

"I've never thought to try to define family, but I guess it's people who live together and care about one another, who look after each other. Gene's gay nephew Craig feels like part of my family, but I'm not sure there is anyone else in the family. We've both had other friends, and I'm always pleased when he can get together with someone else now because there are a lot of things I can't do, at least not very easily.

"We've never had a fight. Occasionally, we've exchanged a few sharp words, but it's been over like that. We might pout for a little bit, but that's about as far as it ever went. Never a screaming fight. Neither of us are very combative. We talk over our differences, although we don't have many, anymore. There are some times I just let him do whatever he wants without taking exception, because I know it's a battle I'll probably lose anyway. Mostly, I don't care. I don't think I would have changed anything. I've been happy with the way things turned out.

"I knew I was not quite like the other boys by the time I was in high school. I think I knew without putting a name to it. I'd heard of Oscar Wilde and so forth at that point. I don't know that I ever thought being gay was wrong. I never felt anyone hated me for being gay, nor did I hate myself for it. And I'd had other relationships before Gene, but never a live-in relationship. The others were less successful; they weren't flings, but we kept separate residences. One I was somewhat obsessed with walked out on me and it upset me very badly, but I was young then and didn't realize there'd be other chances.

"Now that it's getting pretty close to being all over for me, I can say I have no regrets. My favorite memories of Gene, the best times we ever had, were those weekends in Pennsylvania. We ate, went to plays — what was fun was being together. I love a great many things about him: I think he's honorable, and he's as good a friend as anyone could hope for, not only to me, but to many others. He's loyal and has high principles and is devoted to anyone he has cared about.

"It's important to realize that a partner has a life that doesn't necessarily involve you. I've tended to be too possessive sometimes, especially early on. I was 34 when I met Gene. There was a time when I was obsessed with him, and I suppose that was the time when I was too possessive, but we got through that all right.

"People who say that gay people don't have relationships that last are nuts. It's harder for us because there isn't the social force to keep you together. If anything, it's more likely to draw you apart. But it can be done. I know several couples like us."

Gene helps Keith negotiate a walk in their apartment's courtyard.

ON THE ROAD AGAIN

DIANE WHITAKER AND WEEZIE EWING'S FAMILY
Arizona

Build it and they will come. Only the muse is not speaking to a male Midwestern farmer in midlife crisis. This time she reaches the imagination of lesbians retiring from public school teaching and Northeast winters. Recreational vehicle (RV) enthusiasts and women (W), they join together as *RVW* to carve out a home for themselves in the Arizona desert.

RVW started with road rallies and grew to include the acquisition of property. This is a place for older women without men. It is a common scenario. But surely, for most of these women, it is one of choice. This is a new community where women-identified women and lesbians have a home base to park their rigs when they aren't traveling to the South Rim of the Grand Canyon or meeting in the central club house for a potluck. For us younger gay men and lesbians, who have few role models of how to grow old, this is a place of possibility.

Diane picks Jean and me up at the airport in her Saturn stationwagon. There is a long drive filled with warm conversation and a stop for lunch at an Italian restaurant. By the time we arrive, her partner Weezie and a friend are absorbed in a 3-D jigsaw puzzle. It is too late for me to get a tour of the club house. Men are allowed in there, but only from the hours of 11 to 2. So I help with the puzzle while Jean sets up for the interviews.

Later I wander around to find a spot for the group photo. I breathe in the winter desert air which is deliciously dry and subtly seductive. A future beckons.

WEEZIE EWING

63, retired elementary school teacher

"Diane and I have been together 15, 16 years now. We homesteaded in Maine for 13 years. All we had to live on was my retirement, which was nothing. We raised all our own food — pigs, ducks, chickens, turkeys, geese, and gardens. Diane did some massages and then set up a holistic healing center. I ran everything, mowed the lawns, kept track of the funds, and did building and repair, and I had a side business in the wintertime—I had a little snowplow on my tractor and I'd plow people out.

"One morning, six years ago, I couldn't wake Diane up. I got her to the hospital and we discovered she had a fist-sized brain tumor and it had to come out. I realized then we just couldn't keep going with this exhaustion. So I said, 'Guess what? We're closing everything up. We're going to get ourselves a motor home and take six months and go tour the country.' So we found a third-hand motor home and took off. We went all across the country. We got to California to see a friend of

ours, and she had a place in Mexico and wanted us to go down there and spend Christmas with her, so we did that, and then we had a leisurely trip for the rest of the winter.

"I sold the old house in Maine, the one that was in the family for seven generations. It freed me like you wouldn't believe. That place became my mother's prison. I said, 'No way is it going to become my prison.' For 56 years I was not living my own life, I was living my mother's dream. When she hopped over the twig, I said, 'Ma, your dream is my nightmare, and it's gonna stop.'

"But we kept going to these campgrounds where it was Ma and Pa, all heterosexual couples, and they'd all say, 'Are you traveling alone?' We'd say, 'No, we're together.' And they'd say, 'No, where's your old man? Did he die?' We finally decided to tell everybody we were sisters, and widowed, and save the hassle. Then they shut up.

"I kept saying, 'There have to be other women like us, traveling.' I kept looking at travel magazines, and finally I found an ad for RVW, RVing Women — women who liked to RV got together and formed a club, and they travel together in caravans. Diane and I started to go to rallies that they hold where 20 or 30 rigs get together at a campground for a weekend and do all sorts of incredible stuff, like learning about your rig, how

Left to right, in their RV Park are Jean Cameron, Shevy Healey, Ruth Silver, Diane Whitaker, Weezie Ewing, Alta Jones, and Janet Hanson.

The jigsaw puzzle of champions is three-dimensional.

to change the oil, how to make repairs, where the generator is, all this great stuff. Some of them are 45 feet long, and there's a lot that can go wrong in them. And Diane and I really got into it with our funny old rig.

"We were asked to run the rallies on the East coast. In the second year of doing that, I got breast cancer. I had to do six months of chemotherapy after my mastectomy, and we thought that might interfere, but I said, 'No way am I going to throw up,' and I didn't get sick at all. And we kept running the rallies.

"It was two and a half years ago that they sent me home from the hospital with metastatic breast cancer and said, 'Get your things together, because you're going to die in about eight months.' And I said, 'Well, I'm not sure I'm ready to do that.' So here I am, still walking around and feeling terrific.

"I got sober nine years ago, the year after my mother died. I knew I was going to die if I kept going the way I was going. I reached out and asked for help, and two days later I was on a plane to a hospital. I stayed there for 30 days. I have not wanted a drink since. I went to AA meetings almost every night for two years.

"I consider RVW and this community my family. This is where I want to be, this is where they want me to be. I chose this to be my family. I have hardly anybody left, blood-wise, that are family. Just my two cousins. I have others related by blood, but they're not my family. We're all dysfunctional together. Some are still active alcoholics. My brother and I didn't speak for nine years.

"My family here doesn't force me to do anything, except abide by some real down-to-earth, common sense rules for my protection and for theirs. And

they give me unconditional love. At home, love was always conditional. If I did this, I would get that. If I didn't do it, I was a damned brat.

"I have five beautiful grandchildren that are my partner's, but they call me Grandma, and two children who recognize me as being their mother's partner and are just as open and warm and welcoming to me as if I were their own mother.

"I don't identify as old. I'm just a kid, that's what I feel like. I'm doing everything that I wanted to do as a kid and couldn't. I'm looking forward to next October when I'm going to be skippering a boat in the Fiji Islands with a bunch of these women. I get tired, and I have my limitations, but I wake up every morning eager to get going."

DIANE WHITAKER

63, massage therapist

"It never even occurred to me that there was such a thing as lesbians. I knew there were gay men, but I didn't know anything about women. I got married the day out of high school. I wanted children, I wanted family. My first husband died and the second marriage was a disaster. Then I dated for years, going out with different men, and I realized I didn't want to do that anymore, so I said I was going to become celibate.

"Then I found out being a lesbian was a possibility. I went to the National Organization for Women conference in '75 or '76, and as I walked in, Barbara Love was speaking very passionately about the lesbians marching for abortion and doing all the work and now people wanted them to go back in the closet. I'm just standing there with my mouth open. I went to a workshop on sexuality and sensuality where she had diagrams and

everything showing that actually it was more natural and better to have same-sex relationships unless you wanted children. And I said, 'Oh my goodness, isn't that interesting?' So I joined NOW to meet women, and immediately became vice president and newsletter editor and head of three or four task forces. I didn't have any time to have a relationship! But then it came – I had the time and opportunity.

"I've had a very, very strong sex drive throughout my life. My daughter has criticized me for having so many male lovers, and then so many women lovers. I guess it was with her I first said, 'You know, I go into everything just real open. I don't halfway do anything. I can find out faster if it's right or not. And if it's wrong, I change it.' So many people, both heterosexual and homosexual, stay with people forever because they couldn't divide the house or because of the children, or whatever. I just never agreed with that.

"Weezie's just a part of me. At first we were so enmeshed, we even went to the bathroom together! In town, they never saw us apart. I realized that we were enmeshed when I saw a woman who had been with her partner for something like 40 years. A few weeks after her partner died I asked her how she was doing, and she said, 'I'm fine, except half of me is numb.' Someone had said to her, 'Well, of course, half of you died.' They were two halves, trying to make a whole. Well, that's when I came up with the mathematics. We've always said two halves make a whole, but mathematically, two halves make a quarter. And when we realized that, we, in our own bumbly way, tried to disenmesh and become whole individuals. Going into AA helped with that, helped immensely.

"Weezie and I are witnesses for each other in our growth. We've been emotionally frozen little three-year-old children, both of us, and now we're growing up. We're witnessing that, as I think two sisters in a family would. We're sisters and we're lovers and we're friends. We're all of that.

"When I came here, I found people to bounce feelings off of and confirm that what's happening is happening. Before, I just had to figure out everything for myself. And I get touching and hugs. I think I became a massage therapist because I was so touch-deprived. I used to look like I was going to touch my mother, and she would faint. She just couldn't stand being touched.

"I feel like I've always been out of step because I'm way ahead in the holistic things – things I said 20 years ago are just now coming to be. But even if the people here don't agree with me – I'm even further out now – at least they don't shame me or make fun of me. So I can just be me and have fun with what I'm doing. I don't have to have their approval, I just like being with them.

"It's all happening because it's supposed to, and it's an opportunity to learn how to do things differently instead of repeating the past. I'm learning how to first be tender with myself. The more I love myself, the more love I can give to Weezie, to my daughter, to my friends. My work now is releasing not only judgment of myself, but of other people, and we're all learning and trying to figure out how everything works, like putting that puzzle together. Family and friends and others are all pieces, and we're all one."

While on the road, the women of RVW stay in touch with CB radio.

JANET HANSEN

81, retired canoe outfitter and real estate agent

"I had been living in an apartment in Duluth, Minnesota, with a bunch of old people, some of them younger than I am, but very old in their habits. I was bored as hell. Then friends told me about RVW, so I started going to their rallies. And that was a ball.

"At a rally in Austin, Minnesota, I ran into a group that was going to travel from there to the Calgary Stampede. So I went along on it, and there were two ladies from Edmonton, Canada, and they wanted to buy down here in this community. I hadn't even thought about it. I hated the desert; I've always loved the woods. But I met these people, and they were having so much fun! At every caravan, at every rally, I met dynamic women. These women were successful people;

they'd already been past the stages of learning how to do things. And I enjoyed being with them, 'cause I had accomplished in my life what I wanted to do, which was be a successful businesswoman. So when I got out here I decided to buy.

"I've never really met up with anybody like the people in this park. I love a lot of people here. Diane and Weezie are very personal friends. I do a lot of things with them. I went and visited them in Maine this past summer and had a ball with them.

"I haven't been partnered for a long, long time. When I got out here, about five people approached me, looking for partners. I kept saying, 'I'm not available,' because I'm very much set in my ways, and at my age I don't think I want to adapt myself to another person.

"I have to admit there are a lot of people in this park that look up to me. I'm sort of a role model, because of my age, and I do so many things that it

encourages people to keep on doing things they want to do. I'm a feisty little person, and I have lots of fun doing what I'm not supposed to do."

ALTA JONES

59, retired aerospace worker

"Jerry and I got together when I was 22 and she was 29. We've been together 37 years. It took a long time to make a circle of friends 37 years ago, because you weren't out to anybody – no one would admit it.

"Jerry means everything to me, absolutely everything. I wouldn't know what to do without her, she's been a part of my life for so long. I'm the strong one in the family, and yet I can tell you that, emotionally, I'm going to be the one more at a loss than she is.

"The main reason that Jerry and I wanted to be a part of this community was if something happens to one or the other of us, we have a support system. We have someone that's going to understand.

"This is a real quiet, big women's movement. It will grow, it will get bigger, it will get better. It's probably the best thing that has happened for lesbians; to be able to go to your own community and live. And I mean live!"

RUTH SILVER

75, retired social worker

"When I retired, I became very active, doing things for myself. I had always been doing for other people, and I said, 'It's time to think about me instead.' It was the beginning of the best time of my life. All the childrearing and the work responsibilities are over. You're not punching a time clock, you're doing the things that you're doing because you want to do them. And you don't have to do certain things if you don't want to. There's very little pressure. It's a time of great freedom, and a time of wonderful pleasure.

"I lived as a lesbian, prior to my marriage, for 15 years. I didn't marry 'til I was 31, when my lover of four years, who I thought was going to be my life partner, left to marry and have children. I had been in three relationships, one after the other, and that was what happened each time. I thought, 'Well, I'm not going to do this again.' It was just too difficult. So I said, 'If you marry, then I will marry.' I found this sweet man whom I thought would be a fine partner – he was very non-threatening and gentle – and we married. I was married for 39 years. My husband didn't know anything about my previous life as a lesbian.

"My husband and I lived our separate lives. I worked with people all the time, and I immersed myself in cultural activities outside of my work. When I came out to my husband finally, it was a very amiable separation.

"The day Shevy and I moved here, all of our things had been put outside in front of our house. And suddenly a gang of women appeared. I never knew them, I never saw them before. They said, 'We're going to help you take the stuff in, because it's going to rain.' There was no question. They just were there. That's what families are supposed to be."

SHEVY HEALEY

72, retired clinical psychologist

"I looked at my mother and I thought my aging might be like hers. She was so frightened of growing old that she fought it. She was angry about being old, every step of the way. If she lost function in some way, she would be mad at the people around her. There's no question that I've lost some function in terms of memory and sometimes energy. That means I have to find another way of handling things. But I haven't lost the capacity for thought or for feeling. In some ways I think I'm clearer and sharper than I've ever been in my life. It's as though I see things less through projection and more for how they really are. That's pretty exciting. I feel like my life has been a quest to try to figure it out, and this is my last chance to go for it.

"More and more, old lesbians are active. My partner and I traveled around the country for almost two years and met with old lesbians. We had never done this before in our lives. We just said, 'Hey! Now is it!' And we went out and we did it. We met old lesbians and made new friends everywhere we went. We had a grand time, and we ended up here.

"Life didn't stop for us when we got old. The freedom of not having to work for a living is just sensational. We're not accountable in the same way, we're not frightened in the same way, we don't have a boss that we have to please or toady to in order to hold onto a job. So we feel much more in charge of ourselves and our lives.

"Barbara Macdonald [author of *Look Me In The Eye: Old Women, Aging and Ageism*] says that no woman ever got free within the confines of the traditional family, where mother is the servant to both the husband and the children. In that respect, family is the oppressor. This is not an easy question, because, for instance, I have a daughter, a son-in-law, and a grandson; my partner has two

Diane and Weezie leave their rig to take a walk into the sunset.

children. My biological family is important to me. But my family of choice, the family from which I seek and get support, love, interest and stimulation, is my everyday family. I see my daughter two or three times a year. The people I see on a day-in and day-out basis and with whom I celebrate holidays—these are my old lesbian friends.

"Family, at its best, means a group of people who are with you. You're there for them, they for you. There are some issues now in the community in which we live. We have differences. But because we're family, we'll hang in there and hang in there and hang in there and work them out. What that means, then, is that we can count on each other. If I need to go to the hospital, or if I just want to have fun, I can call up and say, 'Let's have a meal together, be together.' When I was having a tooth pulled, Diane came over, wanted to know if she could come to the dentist with me, gave me all kinds of homeopathic remedies. Soon as I was back from the dentist, there she was with a hug. It's wonderful to be in that circumstance. That's family in its most positive and idealistic sense. I can count on them. Isn't that what we really always want from family? And almost never get?

"The family as we know it is dysfunctional, because it doesn't support the kind of interactions that are best for children, best for mothers, and best for fathers. If you've read Margaret Mead, you know that that isn't always the way families are or were, that there are big extended families with three or four women mothering in common, and nobody has the total responsibility.

"I come from a single parent household – there was just my mother and me – so I have always longed to have family. I had a myth about a wonderful, loving family being there for you. It took me a long time to realize it really wasn't my mother's fault that she wasn't there for me. In our society, it's only mother who is there to give. So she never gives enough, she never got enough to start with, and both children and mother are robbed.

"I have never had my need for family met as well as I'm having it met now. Here the relationship is not based on, 'I need, you give', but a much more reciprocal thing which is, 'I'm here for you, you're here for me, we enjoy each other.'

"I don't want to be anybody's grandmother. I don't want to be anybody's mother. I want to be able to sit and talk with them eye to eye about the things I know and they know and we can learn from each other. That's very rare. And here it happens.

"At a certain point as a young woman I said, 'I don't ever want to be in love again. That is not a good state of affairs.' I want to love and be loving, but being in love is sort of a special craziness that has to do with how needy you are and how you think the other person can give you what you don't have yourself.

"Now I have a partner and we share stuff and do stuff together, and it really is a dream come true. Sex is different for me now. It's certainly present, but it is different. Sex used to be involved with lots more lust, lots more power, lots more status, all kinds of things besides sex. I think it's less now, from that perspective. And I think it's got a much greater mix of affection. That doesn't mean it's not exciting, but it's not exciting in the same way for me. There's a sweetness about it, a dearness, that's very special.

"I think retirement means working harder than you ever did in your life and not getting paid. A good part of my life is doing things in and around OLOC, Old Lesbians Organizing for Change. I'm a member of the steering committee, and I spend a lot of time writing articles for the newsletter and handling correspondence. OLOC is the conscience of the lesbian community and the women's movement. We're saying the issue of ageism has not been addressed and we're not going to be invisible any longer. We're not going to put up with it. We want to be included where it counts. How many old lesbians are in positions of any kind of power, any kind of leadership, even any kind of consultantship? We want the notion of empowerment to be part of the agenda. When you characterize us as these 'poor old lesbians' who have been in the closet all their lives, and now they're lonely and suffering and all the rest of it, you're totally overlooking us as vital, exciting, interesting women.

"Particularly in my work in OLOC, the sense of making an impact, of doing important work, of changing society – the sense of substance, if you will – is more present now than any time I can remember. I feel I'm doing something bigger, more important, and that's surprising to me. I thought my old age wouldn't be like my mother's, but neither did I think it would be as grand as it is."

POSTSCRIPT

This book started as a collaboration between a writer and a photographer. Being the latter, I had no expectations of writing my own postscript. But change is the only part of life which is certain, and over the course of a long journey the path can sometimes take an unexpected turn.

Jean Swallow and I were finished with our road trips and we were back in Seattle to complete our work. It was a difficult time and we found ourselves arguing frequently over book-related issues. Our disagreements seemed to get very personal. Still, we continued meeting weekly, going over issues and trying to learn to fight fairly.

On Monday morning, January 16, 1995, Jean missed her 10 o'clock meeting with me and at 10:30 her friend Marian Michener called me from Harborview Medical Center to tell me that Jean had overdosed on aspirin and was in intensive care. Jean died that afternoon at 1 p.m.

The week after Jean's memorial I walked into her office and picked up her papers and tapes. Irena Klepfisz (Chapter 21), a longtime friend, fellow Jewish peace activist and a well known writer, offered to read and comment on the chapter introductions and I jumped at the chance. I asked Betsy Walker (Jean's life partner), Marian Michener (Jean's long-time friend and writing partner), and Beth Healy (who had already been working with Jean on editing the book) to help me complete the project. In weekly meetings over pizza we transcribed and edited and wrote and rewrote, arguing about what Jean would have wanted and how best to present the families that all of us had come to care deeply about. The four of us couldn't replace Jean, but we did manage to complete this book with respect for her vision and the work she had accomplished.

This project was shaped by the way Jean could bring out the best of people when she interviewed them. She was grateful and in awe of everyone she met and everyone instantly trusted her. They told her things I'm sure they never thought to say to anyone else.

Jean's knowledge of publishing and journalism made this book possible. Her skills and enthusiasm made it a reality. She knew how to keep her eye on the prize. She was a great person to collaborate with. I loved her, and will miss her.

—*Geoff Manasse*

EULOGY

Jean asked me once if I would do a eulogy for her, and I agreed, hoping it wouldn't be too soon, and feeling it would be hard to know what to say. But, you know, it comes to you. You may have heard she wrote extensive notes for this memorial several years ago, right down to the arugula salad and the gingerbread. She had given a lot more advance thought to this day than any of the rest of us. When they were working on Jean at the hospital, Monday, I said to my friend Colleen, 'I have a sudden feeling this is like Huck Finn attending his own funeral.' I can picture Jean watching us and doing a running commentary on her friends, and writing up fashion violations.

I've been thinking of this as my last writing assignment from Jean. But since she believed in communication between the living and the dead, and I've had some experience along that line, I'm not so sure. I can hear now how her voice will pop up whenever I contemplate whether to do something difficult. She'll be saying, "Do it. Do it. You can do it."

We've been friends for fourteen years. We met when we were both doing office work in a hospital in San Francisco. She was always a loyal friend. I don't like using the past tense here, because I hope she's right, and our love does survive her death. But there is a mighty change of forms here.

People have talked to me a lot this week about her shameless honesty and the empathy that was almost too much for her at times. And I've felt how lucky I have been to have her as a friend.

A lot of our relationship centered around writing. We did more or less annual readings together in San Francisco and Seattle. Last Friday, Jean and I went to hear a reading by our friend Stan Henry and his friend Cyril Juanitas. Thursday, after Stan and I cried together over Jean's death, he said, "When I chose Cyril to read with me and talked about how much I liked his work, I felt like we were Jean and Marian." I wished I could find Jean to tell her that. And I felt like Burns without Allen, saying "Say goodnight, Gracie," with no one there to deliver the punchline.

Our friendship was very public because we read together and we both wrote about the friendship. Looking back and trying to see what was hidden, I know I had some secret competitions with her that counterbalanced our support, and I suppose the same was true for her. I also know I kept some distance in our friendship because I was suspicious of her hair trigger temper and tendency to fire people from her life. Anger was like an art to her, and it scared me. Though it was great when she was on my side – which she usually was.

We shared many years of sobriety. She quit drinking fourteen years ago, and I quit within the following year. She was proud to have been in Alanon for three years. She was the one who suggested in her unique insistent way that I write about quitting drinking. It's no exaggeration to say she saved my life. And it's breaking my heart that I couldn't save hers.

She contributed a lot to the recovery movement with her two books of writings by lesbians in recovery. Monday, when I started to realize she was going to succeed in killing herself, I couldn't help wondering if the news of this would undermine her contribution. I hope it won't. She was always honest about the fact that recovery is hard work. And that a lot of us quit and find out alcohol wasn't the only thing that made our lives unmanageable. But at least quitting gives us a fighting chance.

Jean never really expected to live past thirty. To her this last decade was a miracle attributable to sobriety and great therapy. I guess we have to be grateful that she made it this long, though it's far too soon for us to let her go. She was always trying to do too much at once. Maybe it was because she expected this early end. The balance between life and death was always precarious for Jean. And her pain went deeper than I wanted to know.

Jean was always proud of making her way without medications like antidepressants. I know that's a common feeling in the recovery community. I'm no psychiatrist. I don't know whether medication would have helped. But if I could have another chance to talk to Jean about it, I would surely say, I would rather have her alive than pill-free. And I'd like to crusade for more support of people doing that if they need to. And for people to talk about suicidal feelings so they can get help.

My other crusade has to do with the fear Jean had of the label Multiple Personality. It may be too reductive or imprecise for the wealth of inner life Jean had. Parts of her had split off as a coping mechanism from major early traumas. I think one of the reasons she killed herself was to protect those personalities from exposure. And another reason was because she was afraid some of them would hurt other people. And it may have been true for Jean, as it sometimes is for people with multiple personalities, that suicide was part of a powerful drive for integration; one of the personalities thought it would survive. I know she was afraid of being stigmatized. She called what was happening to her post traumatic stress syndrome. And she called it intensely imagined inner child work. Whatever we call it, I'd like us to talk with people about what happened here and try to create safer space for someone like Jean to get support to keep doing the hard work of integration, which we all have to do in some form anyway.

Jean did do her work, by the way. She showed up and told the truth. It's like a betrayal of the American dream to find out that wasn't enough.

Friday night, over dinner with our friend Dick before Stan's reading, Jean asked us each to say when was the first time in our lives we really felt different. In her turn, she told the story of going with her father to a mafia barber shop when she was quite small. There she saw a manicurist with high heels, black stockings, a skirt slit to here, red nails, red lips and a black lacquered beehive. When they left the shop, she said, "Daddy, what was that?" And he said, "Well, Jeanie, there are three kinds of females in this world. There are ladies like your mother. There are women like your Aunt Della. And there are babes. That was a babe."

She said she could see she wasn't going to fit into any of those categories. Well, eventually, she figured out she was a lesbian. And one of the things we love about her is that she was, for the most part, a delightfully out lesbian.

Family was important to Jean. The book she just finished is a series of interviews with and photos of gay and lesbian families. It's a beautiful piece of work, and clearly an expression of her quest to name her own family.

Jean was my best person when Cheryl and I got married several years ago. And though she had some criticisms of our relationship, she seemed to feel responsibility for supporting us long after the ceremony was over.

Last year, I was honored to join Jean's friend Gordon, her brother Chan, and Wendy the cousin she thought of as a sister, as witnesses of Jean and Betsy's wedding. It was one of the most moving events in my life. I was impressed by the ways Jean's parents and brother and sister-in-law and aunts and uncles and cousins came and supported Jean and Betsy. I know that brought about an incredible amount of healing in Jean's relationship with her family. It seemed like a miracle in a lot of ways.

Though Jean and Betsy had a lot of struggles, Jean loved her more than anyone. Jean said it was a marriage made in heaven. And you need that when you're going through hell.

Jean's relationships with her stepchildren, Kate and Robin, were tender and important parts of her life. She chose to stay family with Diane, the partner she had first moved to San Francisco with, even after they broke up. And she was very honored to be the godmother to Diane's daughter,

Molly. She also still loved her other exes, Leslie and Sherry. She was proud of her work managing Leslie's medical office, and the support she gave Sherry in her publishing business. And she appreciated the support her exes gave her in her work. She treasured her circle of friends, many of whom are here. She included Cindy, Gordon, Susan, Scott and me among her enduring family.

Jean was very much affected by the loss of several friends to AIDS. Her family book is dedicated, in part, to "the men I loved who had to take the early train home." She volunteered as a driver for people with AIDS at Bailey-Boushay house in Seattle where I'm sure her gallows humor comforted men she only knew for a brief time.

Jean's growing relationship with God was another welcome miracle. I can still see how happy she was when I told her I was starting to learn how to pray. She found solace and community in the Metropolitan Community Church in San Francisco. And she was delighted when she felt welcomed as a member of the Findlay Street Christian Church in Seattle. It meant a lot to her when Pastor Joan Robey told her she didn't have to deny the angel voices she heard. She loved it that they asked her to be a deacon, bad girl that she thought she was. I know she was looking forward to growing with that congregation.

The looking forward stuff is hard. We were going to take a T'ai Chi class together. Friday, she gave me the first five chapters of the family book to proofread and asked me if I could get it back to her on Thursday. I thought we were going to grow old playing bridge together. She was looking forward to going to Costa Rica with Betsy to see their son Robin. She got two Mary Chapin

Carpenter CDs for Christmas and she returned one for the songs of Hilda of Bingen. This is not the way a person acts when she is planning on checking out.

And yet, in recent months, she talked about how much she struggled with suicide. She told me not to be unhappy if she felt she had to do it. Well, of course we're unhappy.

The problem with suicide is that the murderer and the victim are the same person. And so is the executioner. She has already been punished too much. And the rest of us are left wondering who to punch. Or punching pillows.

I guess I'm a woman of many parts, too. And part of me has to trust Jean's angels. Maybe, compared to the pain she was in and didn't see an end to, she made the right decision. I was sitting by the bay, crying, yesterday, and I saw a duck dive and disappear under the water so long I thought she was gone. And I had to smile when she finally bobbed back up. I can't help waiting for Jean to do the same. Say goodnight, Gracie.

— *Marian Michener (Delivered Saturday, January 21, 1995, at Findlay Street Christian Church)*

JEAN SWALLOW is the author of *Leave A Light On For Me*, a novel (Alyson 1991), and the editor of two anthologies, *Out From Under* (Spinsters 1983), and *The Next Step* (Alyson 1993). Her shorter pieces, poems, personal essays, critical reviews, and interviews were published in the mainstream as well as alternative press, both here and abroad. She received a B.A. in Journalism from the University of North Carolina at Chapel Hill, and worked as a journalist, both before and after her degree, for more than twenty-five years, and over those years gathered four writing awards for her interviews.

GEOFF MANASSE lives with his life-partner, Dan Tuttle, in Seattle, Washington. His photos have appeared in *National Geographic*, *Newsweek*, and *Infoworld*, on calendars, and in galleries. He is the winner of the *1992 Northwest Design Awards' Award of Excellence for Photography* and the *1980 Cowles Award* for feature photography presented by the Associated Press.

Photo by Robin Manasse